CAMBRIDGE LIBRARY COLLECTION

Books of enduring scholarly value

History

The books reissued in this series include accounts of historical events and movements by eye-witnesses and contemporaries, as well as landmark studies that assembled significant source materials or developed new historiographical methods. The series includes work in social, political and military history on a wide range of periods and regions, giving modern scholars ready access to influential publications of the past.

A Country Without Strikes

Henry Demarest Lloyd (1847–1928), writer and social reformer, rose to prominence as one of America's first muckraker journalists. Born in New York City, Lloyd started his journalism career at the *Chicago Tribune* and went on to expose the abuse of power in American oil companies. He also pursued a career in politics. In 1899 he travelled to New Zealand and Australia, the 'political laboratories' of Great Britain, to investigate how they resolved the conflict between organised capital and organised labour, and how they promoted social welfare. This book, published in 1900, praises New Zealand's system of compulsory arbitration and describes many instances of successful dispute resolution, from clothing manufacture to newspaper typesetting. The book includes an introduction by William Pember Reeves (1857–1932), liberal newspaper editor and writer, who as New Zealand's minister of labour had brought in the Arbitration Act of 1894 and other important labour legislation.

T0351964

Cambridge University Press has long been a pioneer in the reissuing of out-of-print titles from its own backlist, producing digital reprints of books that are still sought after by scholars and students but could not be reprinted economically using traditional technology. The Cambridge Library Collection extends this activity to a wider range of books which are still of importance to researchers and professionals, either for the source material they contain, or as landmarks in the history of their academic discipline.

Drawing from the world-renowned collections in the Cambridge University Library, and guided by the advice of experts in each subject area, Cambridge University Press is using state-of-the-art scanning machines in its own Printing House to capture the content of each book selected for inclusion. The files are processed to give a consistently clear, crisp image, and the books finished to the high quality standard for which the Press is recognised around the world. The latest print-on-demand technology ensures that the books will remain available indefinitely, and that orders for single or multiple copies can quickly be supplied.

The Cambridge Library Collection will bring back to life books of enduring scholarly value (including out-of-copyright works originally issued by other publishers) across a wide range of disciplines in the humanities and social sciences and in science and technology.

A Country
Without Strikes

*A Visit to the Compulsory
Arbitration Court of New Zealand*

Henry Demarest Lloyd

CAMBRIDGE
UNIVERSITY PRESS

CAMBRIDGE UNIVERSITY PRESS

Cambridge, New York, Melbourne, Madrid, Cape Town,
Singapore, São Paolo, Delhi, Tokyo, Mexico City

Published in the United States of America by Cambridge University Press, New York

www.cambridge.org
Information on this title: www.cambridge.org/9781108039475

This edition first published 1900
This digitally printed version 2012

ISBN 978-1-108-03947-5 Paperback

A COUNTRY
WITHOUT STRIKES.

A COUNTRY WITHOUT STRIKES

A Visit to the Compulsory
Arbitration Court of New Zealand

By

HENRY DEMAREST LLOYD

WITH INTRODUCTION BY
WILLIAM PEMBER REEVES
EX-MINISTER OF LABOR IN NEW ZEALAND

MANUFACTURED IN NEW YORK, U. S. A.

NEW YORK AND LONDON
DOUBLEDAY & McCLURE CO.
21 BEDFORD STREET, W. C.
1900

CONTENTS.

INTRODUCTION

It is very often asserted that those political laboratories, the Colonies of Great Britain, shrink from no experiment the object of which is to regulate and improve the condition of the labourer. This assertion is but partly true. The British colonies, though all endowed with complete self-government, differ very widely in the temper in which they approach the labour problem. For instance, two of the knottiest questions which humanitarian social reformers have endeavoured in our time to solve, are confessedly the conflict of organised capital with organised labour, and the necessity of securing a minimum of comfort for the humbler class of workers. Among eleven self-governing British colonies two only have made any serious endeavour to cope with the second of these problems, and one only has made any determined effort to grapple with the first. Victoria and New Zealand essay to control by statute wages and the conditions of labour; in New Zealand alone the conflicts of labour and capital are by law and custom submitted to the arbitration of state tribunals. The Victori-

an Factories' Act, to which I have just referred,
is an extremely interesting measure under which
the wages paid and certain other conditions
observed in the clothing, boot and shoe, furni-
ture-making, and one or two other industries
are determined from time to time by a state
board whose rulings have legal force.   The
statute deserves careful study and may be regarded as an experiment kindred to, though by
no means identical with, the New Zealand Industrial Conciliation and Arbitration Act which
is the subject of Mr. Lloyd's book.   There are
theorists and observers in Great Britain who
think that the Victorian law is more likely to be
imitated in the large industrial countries of the
world than that of New Zealand, and that its narrower scope and more calculable effects render
it a less venturesome and hazardous experiment.
There is no doubt something to be said for this
contention if the object of the reformer be merely to better the conditions of the most helpless
class of workers in the worst-sweated industries.
But if the object be to find a remedy also for
those conflicts of capital with labour which have
agitated the industrial world in Europe, America and elsewhere for the past century, which increase in area and bitterness with each decade
and which constitute one of the greatest puz-
zles of social students in the old world and the
new, then the Victorian Wages Board law is
not what is wanted.

The object of the New Zealand Conciliation
and Arbitration Act is not only to stamp out
sweating and improve the workers' condition.

These, indeed, were not its immediate aims
though they are consequences—and very valuable consequences—which have flowed from it.
Its special and primary object was to bring
about industrial peace, and, in so far as it has
substituted orderly and methodical hearing and
adjudication by impartial state tribunals for the
loose, violent and haphazard methods of the
strike and the lockout, it has succeeded in bringing about industrial peace.

True it is that an act under which one of
the parties to an industrial dispute has the
right to bring all other parties before a public tribunal does, in effect, if general use be
made of it, involve a great deal of state
regulation of labour. That is what has come
about in New Zealand, and those who look
upon state interference as anathema, and think
that any law which increases it is necessarily bad, will regard the arbitration law with
abhorrence. So far, however, as New Zealand is concerned, a sufficient answer to this
objection is easily found. In the first place,
if the parties to labour disputes there wish to
settle their own differences in their own way,
the state does not meddle with them. In the
second place, New Zealand is perhaps the most
simple and complete little democracy in the
world; legislation is facile, and were any law
found tyrannical or intolerable it would have
very short shrift indeed. In New Zealand, I
may remark, the most powerful class in politics
are not the wage-earners but the farmers.

The Arbitration Act has not yet had a very

long life. It was passed in 1894 and did not come into active use until more than twelve months afterwards. Its popularity and usefulness have, however, steadily increased, and most of the organised industries of the colony are now being carried on under the conditions laid down by its Conciliation Boards and Arbitration Court. It should be stated frankly that most of the cases brought before these tribunals have been initiated by trade-unions and that most of the decisions have granted concessions of more or less value to the plaintiffs. The explanation of this is found in the prosperity which has marked the last four or five years in New Zealand. The labour market has been a rising market since the Arbitration Act came into use. Under the old conditions the workers whose wages had been cut down in the dull times of the previous decade would have struck on a rising market as they strike elsewhere. Instead of striking on a rising market they have arbitrated on a rising market, and instead of the industries of New Zealand being convulsed and disorganised the factories have not been closed through labour troubles for one single day.

Next to the wide use which has been made of the law in the colony, the most striking feature of its history has been the respect that has been paid to its decisions. Where, as in certain cases, these have been disappointing to the trade-unions they have been loyally obeyed; and though in a few instances the same cannot be said for the employers, the recalcitrants have not been many, they have not been employers of great size or standing, and their attempts at resistance or evasion have been sufficiently dealt with by small fines and very moderate penalties.

The only serious argument—beyond the theoretical objection to state interference in any form—which has been brought against the law by English writers has been a statement that it has hampered enterprise and checked the growth of manufactures in the colony. New Zealanders know this to be quite baseless, for they know that the manufactures of their colony have fully participated in the prosperity of the last quinquennium. For some years past, labour in almost every trade has been fully employed, the numbers of the workless have fallen progressively, fresh factories have been opened, fresh buildings erected, and the shopkeepers who deal with the working classes admit that business is better and bad debts fewer than at any time in the last twenty years in the colony. The annual reports of the Chambers of Commerce and the periodical reviews of trade and business published by the New Zealand newspapers on both sides in politics tell the same tale. But the briefest and most convincing argument for disabusing the mind of any one who may fancy that the New Zealand Arbitration Act has hampered industry is to be found in the following figures which give the hands employed in the registered factories of the colony for the last five years. It may be explained that "factory" in New Zealand means workshop, small or large, and that registration is universal.

Year.	Hands Employed.	Increase.
1895	29,879	4,028
1896	32,387	2,508
1897	36,918	4,531
1898	39,672	2,754
1899	45,305	5,633

It may be, and indeed, has been, stated that the strength of the law cannot be fully tested until some powerful organisation of labour or capital defies the decision of the court and is successfully dealt with. English doctrinaire critics lay great stress on this and are wont to ask triumphantly what could be done with the members of a large trade-union without funds to enable them to pay the court's penalties for disobedience and at the same time stubbornly determined not to go to work under the conditions laid down by the court. The answer to that is surely found in a study of the history of labour disputes. These show that it is not unions destitute of funds which carry on stubborn and ultimately successful strikes. And if impecunious workers cannot successfully cope with the antagonism of employers whose resources are after all limited, how can they expect to cope with the power of a state tribunal whose will is not to be bent, which has no factory to be closed or business to be injured, and which is backed by the forces of law and public opinion?

To my mind, however, the best recommendation of the New Zealand law is just that it has not, so far, led to any desperate trial of strength of this kind. By applying the good old motto that prevention is better than cure it has taken labour disputes in hand before they have reached that pitch at which the passions of the disputants on both sides are inflamed and impel them to wild speech and wilder action; it gets at labour and capital before they have come to the unreasonable stage of their quarrel. It frankly accepts their two irresistible tendencies in modern times; the first of which is that they will differ and the second that they will organise in order to settle their differences. There are philanthropists who think that the remedy for their conflicts is found in urging them not to quarrel and not to organise; there are some who would sternly forbid them to organise. The New Zealand law, on the contrary, frankly encourages their organisation, admits that they are bound to differ, and only insists that if they cannot settle their differences in a friendly and peaceable manner they must go to the state, which will provide them with machinery for doing so.

The state, in New Zealand, is the people, and the people being vitally interested in labour battles, has surely the right to say to the parties that their disputes shall be adjusted in such a manner as not to damage the community of which they are members and for the benefit of which in the end their industry is carried on.

For the rest, the Act's methods are elastic, and the proceedings of its tribunals are open, painstaking and fair.

I am, of course, in no way responsible for the views expressed by Mr. Lloyd in this

volume.   Before Mr. Lloyd went to New Zealand, I had never seen him, and it was not until
he had been to the colony and returned from it
with his views upon the Arbitration Act fully
formed, that I had the pleasure of meeting him.
But though his opinions are his own, I may be
allowed to say that, as regards his statements
on matters of fact, I believe them to be correct
throughout.   In America and Europe his standing as a writer will, of course, ensure his book a
welcome among all social students; and both in
Great Britain and the colonies I feel no doubt
that those who are interested in the experiment
he here describes will gladly welcome the impartial opinion of an able American observer standing absolutely apart from the political parties of
New Zealand.

W. P. REEVES.

LONDON, ENGLAND, March, 1900.

A COUNTRY
WITHOUT STRIKES.

A COUNTRY WITHOUT STRIKES

CHAPTER I.

SOMETHING NEW IN STRIKES AND LOCKOUTS.

WHEN I landed in New Zealand in February, 1899, I found it, like the rest of the world, in the flooding tide of a new prosperity; the revenue of the government increasing, manufactures extending, new enterprises starting, labour busy.

As always happens in a country so fortunate as to have workingmen intelligent enough to know what is going on, those here knew about this rising market and were striking everywhere for their share of it. They were demanding more wages, shorter hours, better conditions, or at least the restoration of advantages which had been taken from them during the preceding years of "the lean kine."

I knew, of course, by my reading, something about the new way these things were managed here, and almost my first request was to be taken

to see a New Zealand strike.   My friend smiled
and led the way.   We were driven to a charm-
ing spot in Christchurch, bordering on "The
Domain," or public park on the banks of the
Avon where English willows turn their hoar
leaves to a stream as beautiful as its namesake.
We approached an interesting Gothic building
which did not look like a factory or trades-union
hall, and passed into a long, open room, with
vaulted ceilings, galleries, stained glass windows, all familiar to any one who has been in
the Parliament buildings at Westminster.   It
was a New Zealand miniature of the House of
Commons—the Hall of the Provincial Assem-
bly of Canterbury.

A table ran along the centre of the hall; on
each side of it three or four men, the brighter
toilets and the better grooming of those on one
side showing them to belong to a different class
from those on the other, whose plain clothing
and furrowed faces bespoke them to be workingmen.   They were busy in controversy, and between them, at the head of the table in the white
wig of an English chief-justice, was a judge of
the Supreme Court of New Zealand.   On
benches under the windows were newspaper re-
porters, and a number of spectators belonging
evidently to the same classes of society as the
men sitting beside each other at the table.

I know a strike when I see it, for I have witnessed a good many, including the Pullman strike at Chicago, but this looked like no meeting of strikers I had ever known. It looked like a court, though, again, not like any I had ever seen before.

But it was both. "For five years," said my New Zealand friend, "there has not been a strike or a lockout in New Zealand that has not been held in a court-room."

This was my introduction to the Compulsory Arbitration law of New Zealand.

"But compulsory arbitration, you know," said a young Englishman who was with us, fresh from Oxford and post-graduate courses of political economy from John Stuart Mill to Boehm-Bawerk, "is an impossibility; it is a contradiction in terms. You cannot make men work whether they want to or not, you cannot compel men to arbitrate nor fix prices by law. You cannot get practical decisions in business matters from judges who 'know nothing of business,' you cannot settle wages and conditions of labour by laws of the legislature instead of the laws of supply and demand."

"That 's what all 'the authorities' of the business world and political economy say," our New Zealander replied, "but what they say we can't do, we are doing. Under this law, when without it they would have stopped, for five years not a workingman nor capitalist has stopped giving or taking work on account of any difference as to wages, or any other matter at issue between them, and yet during all that time they have been in sharp and frequent disputes on many questions."

"The New Zealanders must be a nation of visionaries," the Oxford man insisted, "to be willing to venture on such a Utopian experiment."

"On the contrary, 'the experiment,' instead of being a scheme of visionaries, or Utopians, or theorists, was forced upon us by the hard pressure of actual facts and by intolerable evils, in the paralysis of industry and the disturbance of peace, for which all other remedies have failed.   The experiment was entered upon with the consent substantially of all parties in Parliament, including some of the most successful business men in the colony.   It is an experiment, we admit, and a bold one, without parallel anywhere else in the world, but it is a successful experiment, and so far has done lots of good and hurt nobody."   The traveller is not in New Zealand very long before he finds out that its people are a little proud of their "experiments," and it takes him only a little while longer to make up his mind that they have good reason to be proud of them.

"With your Conciliation and Arbitration Boards, public and private, and your Conseils des Prud'hommes and the like," continued our friend, "you are all saying to the warring forces of labour and capital, 'you ought to arbitrate.' New Zealand is the first to say, 'If you ought to arbitrate, you shall arbitrate.'"

The newly arrived traveller hardly knows which way to turn, there are so many novelties to see in a country like New Zealand. Its whole career has been a continuous experiment, from zoological to sociological, and it has been specially experimenting in business and politics for thirty years, ever since Sir Julius Vogel, in 1869, established the government in life insurance, which it has made a great success against the competition of the principal private companies of Australia, Europe and America. But the statements my New Zealand friend whispered to me, as we stood under the gallery of the Arbitration Court, decided me that compulsory arbitration had the first claim on my curiosity.

New Zealand had a terrible strike nine years ago, known as the Maritime Strike. It devastated the whole of Australasia. It was a war between classes, the only two classes practically which remain to be amalgamated in modern society. It spread from the shipping world, where it began, into a great circle of related industries. Merchants and their clerks drove drays and loaded and unloaded merchandise; shipowners and their sons and friends took the place of sailors and stokers; the country went to the edge of civil war. The New Zealand Minister of Labour, the Honourable William Pember Reeves, set himself, in the following year, to find a remedy to prevent the recurrence of struggles not less terrible in the sum-total of losses than war itself. There had been no compulsory arbitration anywhere to serve as a guide; there had been no public conciliation or arbitration in New Zealand itself to supply any precedent. "But New Zealand," the New Zealander who was giving me these points continued, with pardonable pride, "did not waste any time in beginning where others had begun. It took up the evolution where the others had dropped it, and carried it forward. It was characteristic of the country that the new opportunity found the new men fit for it."

The Maritime Strike was over, but other coming labour troubles clouded on the horizon, and, most threatening of these, a possible strike of the government employés on the railroads. This, as the Minister of Labour said to Parliament, all must admit, would be the greatest possible calamity that could befall.

With the memory of the Maritime Strike before him and these other dangers threatening, the Minister of Labour set himself to study the most difficult of labour problems. He investigated all that has been done in other countries —in England, France, Germany, the Australian Colonies and the United States. The speeches in which he reported the results of his studies to Parliament in introducing the bill which he framed, stand to-day as the best study which has been made of arbitration and conciliation. He found, as he said in offering his bill, that the experience of other countries, confined as it had been to voluntary conciliation and arbitration, was a record of failure wherever it was most important that it should succeed, and of success only when success was comparatively of little consequence. Almost never was any great strike settled or prevented by voluntary conciliation and arbitration; only the little ones.

He read all that has been written by the authorities on conciliation and arbitration, and found nothing new in them. They all seemed, he said, to have copied from each other.

He reviewed for Parliament and the New Zealand public the three laws of Great Britain, passed in 1824, 1867, and 1872, all three dead letters on the statute book.

The Conseils des Prud'hommes of France, which have had eighty years of practical working, are a valuable example of what may be done by state intervention in industrial matters, but they have not put an end to strikes.

"There are many and grievous strikes in France, because these Conseils des Prud'hommes are not allowed to deal with strikes or wages and have no power to enforce their decisions."

He found the Massachusetts Board of Conciliation and Arbitration one of the most successful and practical tribunals in the world. It was in fact almost "an ideal tribunal, its one fault being that it is voluntary. It does a great deal of good, but if you look through the record of its cases, you will find a doleful and depressing list of failures as well. In small cases the intervention of the board had been successful, that is, if passion has not been roused. In larger cases, or where one side has had its passion roused, the board has not been so successful, and the strikes have had to go on." But he found it "the one voluntary state tribunal that seems to do good work."

Mr. Reeves studied his subject for years. He told the Parliament there was not an industrial conciliation and arbitration tribunal in any part of the world, the working of which he had not examined. His conclusion was, "that in England, throughout Europe, in America, and in Australia, voluntary arbitration has failed for generations. It is necessary to try something else, and I ask you to try compulsory arbitration."

A very striking instance of the failure of voluntary arbitration was furnished by the recent experience of the neighbouring colony of New South Wales. That colony had, the year before New Zealand acted, passed an act which seemed to be, Mr. Reeves said, "a very nice act." Immediately thereafter New South Wales saw the three most disastrous and ruinous strikes the colony had had since its foundation. These strikes took place as soon as the act was passed, and it proved a dead letter. If the act had not been passed, these strikes would have compelled the Legislature of New South Wales to legislate in an effectual way, but, as it was, the leaders had a reason in the existence of the law for doing nothing. As a result of these three strikes, the Coal Miners' Strike, the Broken Hill Strike, and the Shearers' Strike, homes had been broken up, employers ruined, the town of Broken Hill made bankrupt, men had lost their homes and their work, their families had been disrupted, labour leaders had been thrown in jail, to be kept there for years, and a very bitter class feeling excited which still rages throughout New South Wales.

"That," said Mr. Reeves, "has been the result of trusting to voluntary tribunals."

He showed that, at the time he was speaking, there had been in Europe in the preceding five years nearly two thousand strikes, and throughout the world at large many thousands of strikes involving the loss of hundreds of millions of dollars, besides other things not to be counted in money. In proposing compulsory arbitration, he said:

"I could not bring in a bill of a weaker character than this without knowing that it would be a hollow sham. I have studied the history of conciliation and arbitration in the various countries of the world, both old and new, and I have been forced to this conclusion that, if you pass a merely optional measure, you will put a thing on the statute book that will have no effect whatever in assuaging the evils arising through industrial contests. Only too thankful should I be to pass an optional measure now, and thus save myself all the friction attending this fight, and also save myself the great responsibility of passing a measure with a compulsory clause, but I cannot pass a useless bill."

"Strikes," he said again, "have done a great deal of good, but strikes are war. War is a clumsy and barbarous way of settling differences between nationalities, and strikes are the most clumsy and barbarous way I know of settling industrial difficulties."

"Victory by either side is not a proof that the side which lost was wrong, or that that which won was right."

The trade-unions of New Zealand, during the discussion of this matter which was before Parliament for years, held up the hands of the Minister of Labour by passing resolutions demanding compulsion, and many of the leading capitalists and employers of the colony gave him their support.

He quoted to Parliament a telling remark made to him by a Manchester merchant, a man who had had great experience in connection with unions.

"If you are to have arbitration at all, it would be of no use, if you do not make the awards compulsory. Every man who thinks he is going to lose a strike is ready to go to arbitration, while the man who thinks he is going to win will not have it."

Conciliation boards are virtually useless unless there is in the background an arbitration court, and this court must have compulsory powers.

That the bill which he drafted was an experiment, "an absolute experiment," Mr. Reeves admitted. He claimed only, he said, that "It was an honest attempt to solve the most difficult of labour problems. It is an experiment that is worth trying.   Whatever it does,.it cannot do a vast amount of harm to the colony."

The opponents of the bill had said that such a question must not be dealt with in an experimental way.

"In Heaven's name," replied Mr. Reeves, "if we are not to deal with it in an experimental way, how are we to deal with it at all?"

"Every good and great change in the world has been an experiment.   The man who discovered America made an experiment.   Every great scientific invention has been arrived at by experiment, and, in the same way, in legislation we have to make experiments."

The Minister of Labour admitted the imperfections of this bill.   "It is ridiculous," he said, "to suppose that at one bound this Parliament can solve a problem that has puzzled the most earnest thinkers for generations."   But he believed that, if the experiment had a fair trial, it would succeed, and that "New Zealand will have set an example to the civilised world which will be widely followed in days to come."

Mr. Reeves submitted his first bill to Parliament in 1892.   It was offered again in 1893 and in 1894.   Three times it passed the lower house before the upper house would allow it to become a law.   So convincingly had the Minister of Labour marshalled the results of his studies of conciliation and arbitration in other countries, and defended his main point that compulsion was indispensable, that the bill at last, in 1894, passed without change in its fundamental principles, and with the concurrence of the leader of the opposition and several of its most important members—a most unusual circumstance in a country where party spirit runs as high as it does in New Zealand.

"I believe," the leader of the opposition said, "that we have to a great extent the very best bill that can be devised in the interest of the colony."

The act has now been in operation five years, and with such general approval that recent amending acts have been passed almost without dissent. The law was proposed as an experiment —it is still regarded as an experiment by its author, and even by the judges of the Arbitration Court and by the country—but so far it has proved a workable experiment.

There has not been a strike by organised labour, with one insignificant exception, since its passage. It has harmonised all the labour troubles brought under its cognisance. The courts have been constantly strengthening themselves and the acts by their administration of it. Capital has not fled, but, on the contrary, industries of all kinds have been flourishing as never before. There have been a few attempts to evade or disregard the decisions of the courts; these the judges have proved themselves fully able to control and punish. Although the decisions have almost all been in favor of the men, because it is a time of prosperity and their demands have been made on a rising market, the employers have found no serious embarrassment in complying with them, and some of the employers are the strongest supporters of the measure.

To declare a new social right and to create a new court to enforce it in a field where there was nothing to guide and nothing to be copied, and where, still worse, all the authorities deny the right and predict complete failure for the enforcement, was certainly as bold a venture as reformer entrusted with power ever attempted. Merely to draft so unprecedented a law with such skill that it could go into practical operation as this has done, is a legislative feat of the highest order.

Speaking of the pains he had taken, Mr. Reeves told Parliament, "I have had this bill drafted, and in some cases re-drafted, and drafted and drafted again and again."

A law essaying compulsory arbitration in South Australia has been on the books about the same time as the New Zealand law and remains a dead letter, not a single case when I was there having been tried under it.

The lawyer, journalist, poet, politician, who, as Minister of Labour, had the wit to contrive a measure which could give five years industrial peace to his country, is not likely to be assigned a back seat among social inventors. However his experiment may turn out, it is certainly one of the most original pieces of work done in modern times.   But if the "experiment" ripens into an established institution, no one will be able to dispute the claim of Mr. Reeves to stand in the front rank of the geniuses who have proved themselves able to affect human destiny for good, by carrying constitutional and political development a step farther, bettering the life of man with man by bringing new evils under the dominion of the old principles of social justice and mercy.

When I asked Mr. Edward Tregear, the accomplished Secretary for Labour, who has the congenial task of carrying on the work Mr. Reeves began, for a copy of the Compulsory Arbitration Law, he handed me a bulky pamphlet entitled "The Labour Laws of New Zealand."

The arbitration law has to be studied in several acts contained in this collection.   There is an urgent need of a consolidation act for these various enactments, and for want of it the task of accurately ascertaining the definite provisions of the law is a complicated one.

Its main points are:

1. It applies only to industries in which there are trade-unions.

2. It does not prevent private conciliation or arbitration.

3. Conciliation is exhausted by the state before it resorts to arbitration.

4. If conciliation is unsuccessful, the disputants must arbitrate.

5. Disobedience of the award may be punished or not at the discretion of the court.

The compulsion of the law is threefold: compulsory publicity, compulsory reference to a disinterested arbiter—provided the disputants will not arbitrate voluntarily—compulsory obedience to the award.

It does not forbid nor prevent disputes, but makes the antagonists fight their battles in court according to a legal code instead of the ordinary "rules of war."

There is no "making men work by law," and no "fixing wages by law." The law says only that if they work, it must be without strikes or lockouts, and that, if they cannot agree as to prices, the decision shall be left to some impartial person, and not fought out.

In fuller detail these are the principal features of the law.

The state takes no initiative in setting arbitration in motion. The law acts only as one party or the other calls for it—and in this the New Zealand law differs from that of South Australia. It simply provides the law and the tribunal by which either party, employer or employed, may sue and be sued instead of striking or being struck.

The Minister of Labour in submitting the bill avowed himself to be in favour of giving the state an initiative, but he thought that the people were not yet ready for it. I found that where, as in South Australia, the arbitration law gives the officials of the state the power to intervene of their own motion, nothing has been done. But in New Zealand, where the people must initiate whatever is done, the law has been in constant use.

No disputes can be considered except in trades where there are trade-unions, and only where these trade-unions have registered under the law. This is, first, to save the court from being overwhelmed by a flood of petty matters, and, second, because the disputes that threaten the peace and prosperity of society come from organised not unorganised labour.

"On the whole," Mr. Reeves said, "history

shows that the great and dangerous battles between capital and labour—those which may seriously call for state intervention—occur only where labour is organised."

There is in this no disregard of the interests of the poorest and most numerous labourers—the unorganised—for any seven men can form a trade-union under the act and claim all its privileges, nor is it in disregard of the interests of men in a trade who are outside the union, for, as will be explained later, there is a way in which their grievances can be espoused by the union in their trade.   To encourage workingmen and capitalists to organise unions, they are given corporate rights; they can sue and be sued; they can recover subscriptions from defaulting members, and have power to buy or lease land.   The law does not interfere with the right of labour and capital to settle disputes by private arbitration, if they wish to do so.   On the contrary, it supplies forms for procedure in such cases and provides for the enforcement of the awards, if the parties agree in advance that this shall be done.

There are two kinds of tribunals: Boards of Conciliation and a Court of Arbitration, and in both the workingmen and the employers are equally represented by men of their own choice. There is a Board of Conciliation in every "industrial district," and the country is divided into as many industrial districts by the Governor-General as seems advisable.   There is but one Court of Arbitration for the whole country.

The Boards of Conciliation have four to six members, and are chosen every three years in each district by elections held separately by the associations of employers and the association of employés, under procedure carefully arranged by law, and under the supervision of a government officer called the Clerk of Awards.   The boards upon organisation elect as chairman an outsider, " some impartial person," and "willing to act."   The chairman votes only in case of a tie.

The Court of Arbitration consists of three persons who hold for three years, appointed by the Governor-General, and of the three appointees, one must be chosen by him from men nominated by the workingmen, and one from among men nominated by the capitalists.   The third is a Judge of the Supreme Court.   This democratic representation of labour and capital insures to each throughout the proceedings that their interests are protected by men of their own class, familiar with the conditions of their life and industry.   It insures that the casting vote of the chairman is given with men by his side to make clear all the technicalities and difficulties of the questions at issue.

The selection of a Judge of the Supreme Court to preside and to give the final and decisive vote, satisfies the contestants and the people that the state, on its side, contributes to the inquiry and the decision the best that it has of dignity, experience and impartiality.

If the question before the board or court is of more than usual complexity, two experts may be chosen by the two parties to act as full members of the court, and to see that the decision is made with full understanding of all the points. Experts are frequently called in in this way. For special emergencies there may be special boards elected.

Neither board nor court intervene in any dispute of their own motion, but like other courts only when one of the parties or both appears before them.   The compulsion in the law is not that the state of itself compels the parties to arbitrate, but that if one desires to arbitrate instead of fighting, the state says the other must not fight but arbitrate.

The moment either side with a grievance, or any apprehension of a strike or lockout, summons the other before the board or court, it becomes a punishable offence for the workmen to stop work, or the employer to close down.

Both must keep on until the board or court has come to a final decision.

The law goes beyond this prohibition of strikes or lockouts while disputes are pending before the court. There must be no strike or lockout beforehand to forestall such intervention. The act guards against the probability that workingmen might be discharged, or the employer be left by his men because one side has learned that the other is about to demand conciliation or arbitration. In such cases, if there has been any such discharge or lockout to evade an arbitration, the aggrieved party may, at any time within six weeks after the strike or the lockout, appeal to the court and get full consideration and redress, and the court can stop the strike which it was denied the chance to prevent.

The necessity for such action as this was shown in a case which arose in South Australia, where certain workingmen resolved to try arbitration, but the employer getting wind of what was coming, promptly discharged all his hands. He then said to the court that it had no jurisdiction because there was no dispute between him and his men, meaning the men he had taken on afterwards. "It is quite true," he said, "that I had a dispute with certain men, but they are no longer my employés." This New Zealand clause gives the state power, if invoked, to step in and stop strikes or lockouts, even though they have broken out.

Employers can summon their workingmen only as members of a trade-union, but the men can call in individual employers as well as associations of employers; otherwise these could defeat the act by refusing to organise into associations. If the labourers or capitalists choose to sacrifice the benefits of the act by giving up their unions, they can do so, but only in ways provided by law, and not during the progress of any arbitration nor to escape compliance with an award. Workingmen can leave their unions only by giving three months' notice.

Both the Boards of Conciliation and the Court of Arbitration have summary powers of visiting any premises and questioning any persons concerned in an industrial dispute. They can compel the attendance of witnesses and the production of any books and papers needed, and can imprison anyone refusing to obey their summons. Every precaution is taken by the act to prevent injurious publicity of the secrets of business. Usually the hearings are public, so that public opinion may be properly informed, but the court can at any time, at its own discretion, or the request of any of the parties, go into secret session.

No lawyer is allowed to appear before the

boards or the court, except by consent of both parties, which is practically never given.

The Boards of Conciliation have no other powers than those of investigation, visitation, and intermediation.

The proceedings before the boards and the court are very simple, informal, cheap, and expeditious. The board is required to make its decisions within two months, the court within one month after the investigation begins. An association of employers or workingmen wishing to summon a trade-union, makes an application on a printed blank to the board in writing, which thereupon takes up the case.

"The board can make all such suggestions and do all such things as appear right and proper to secure a fair and equitable settlement."

The Boards of Conciliation can make decisions, but the decisions are not binding, and it is the successful party, therefore, who must appeal to the Court of Arbitration.

The Court of Arbitration is a court with ordinary and extraordinary powers. It can summon any party to a dispute which is before it to appear, and, if he refuses, can proceed without him. It can enter and investigate any premises and question any persons there without warrant. It can permit any party who might appear to have a common interest in the matter to be joined in the proceedings. It can receive such evidence as it thinks fit "whether strictly legal evidence or not." It has the power of other magistrates to take evidence at a distance. None of its awards can be set aside for any informality; it is required that they be not framed in a technical manner. They cannot be "challenged, appealed against, reviewed, quashed, or called in question by any court of judicature on any account whatsoever."

The board is to make its decision "according to the merits and substantial justice of the case," and the Court of Arbitration "in such manner as they find to stand with equity and good conscience."

The members of the board and courts are paid moderately only while sitting and witnesses are compensated for the loss of time and for their travelling expenses, but no costs are to be allowed in any case whatever for any agent, counsel or solicitor to appear for either party. The fees and travelling expenses of members of the court are met out of the general funds of the colony. It is felt to be better public policy that the whole community should bear this than to run the risk that poor men might suffer injustice because they could not afford the expense of appealing for justice. The expenses of witnesses are charged as costs to the disputing parties.   It has been proposed that the compensation of the members of boards and the court be always charged to the disputants in order to prevent trivial and excessive litigation, but this has been negatived for the reason of public policy just given.

To check frivolous and causeless appeals to it, the court is authorised to dismiss any such cases and to assess all costs upon the offender.

Business men are protected from the injustice of being put to a disadvantage, perhaps ruinous, by an award giving their employés pay, hours or concessions which their competitors do not have to give.   There is a provision by which all the employers in the district, or in the whole country, if the court so decide, can be brought in and made parties to the procedure and subject to the award.

All trade-unions concerned can be similarly brought in.   Any employer or association of employers, and any trade-union, although not summoned but wanting to appear, may be admitted by the court.

The court can adjust its decisions to the circumstances of the district or country at large, and can vary them as it thinks proper with regard to individuals or trades to secure fair play for all.

An award settles wages or other conditions
in question for two years, if a shorter time is
not specified by the court.   Any person joining
any union or association may be made subject
to any award which has been previously rendered affecting it.

Any workman may stop work and any employer shut down during arbitration or after
an award, provided he can show the court that
he did so for some good reason, such as the un-
profitableness of the business—any reason other
than to escape or defeat its jurisdiction.   But
if he wants to resume during the life of the
award, he can do so only by obeying all its
terms.   The law cannot be evaded or ignored.
Employers cannot escape it by refusing to organise, for they can be brought up singly.   They
can refuse to attend only at the same risk as
in other courts of having the case go against
them by default.   If they refuse to exercise
their right of electing representatives on the
boards and the court, the state does it for them.
The workmen in any trade can keep themselves
out of reach of the law by neglecting to organise, but they would have to be practically unanimous in this, for any seven of them could form
a union and bring every one else concerned, employers and employés, organised or not, before
the court.

Violation of an award is not necessarily an

offence. It is left to the court to decide whether such a breach shall be punished or not. Of course, as a matter of fact, the court does as a rule make disobedience of the award an offence and punishable. But with a practical foresight, which in a new field like this looks much like genius, the author of the law left this matter within the discretion of the court.

"The court," said Mr. Reeves, "might make an award which possibly any employer would rather break than attempt to carry out. It might make an award that members of unions would be prepared to go to prison rather than obey, and under these circumstances the best thing is to leave it to the good sense of the court. We cannot picture to ourselves the infinite diversity of cases that will come before the court. There will be many awards that can be made binding and some which it would be folly to make binding."

Trifling with the awards is likely to prove an expensive amusement. The court determines for itself what constitutes a breach and does not have to define this in advance at the time of making an award. It may, at any time during the life of its decision, adjudge any obnoxious thing which has been done to be a violation of its award, and may punish it. This is as broad as the powers of courts in contempt cases.

A penalty running up to twenty-five hundred

dollars may be imposed for violation of an award.   No more than this can be laid on any party and no more than this can be exacted under any award from all the parties to it.

"In addition to that," Mr. Reeves explains, "the court has the ordinary power of proceeding by committal or attachment against any one who defies it.   This power would be used very reluctantly and sparingly, should all other means fail.   Public opinion generally would support it.   On the other hand, it is not likely to be required."

One fine of twenty-five hundred dollars then would exhaust all the powers of punishment by fine under one award, but a business men's association, trust or monopoly, or a great trade-union, thinking to secure immunity for a continued violation by one payment of twenty-five hundred dollars, would be easily made subject to a new award and to as many more awards as might be necessary to make them good citizens.

"No one could by simply paying a single fine," says Mr. Reeves, "snap his finger thereafter at the court.   He could, of course, be brought before it again and again, and might have to pay fines until he was tired."

The order of the court for such a fine may be filed in the other courts and becomes enforceable as a judgment.   If the property of a trade-union or association of business men is not sufficient to pay the fine, the individual members are liable, but only to the amount of fifty dollars each.

Through a defect in the law at first the only punishment for a violation of the terms of a decision that could be enforced was imprisonment. This was felt to be so harsh a method of dealing with behaviour but newly made legally penal, that the judges evaded it by taking advantage of every possible technicality, and the workingmen, even where they felt themselves aggrieved, would not ask for the infliction of so severe a punishment. The law has now been changed so that the money penalty can be enforced, and the judges show no hesitation in applying it, and the offenders show no hesitation in submitting.

Many of the disputants, knowing that there is an appeal to the Court of Arbitration and determined to take advantage of it, make their appearance before the Conciliation Board little more than a formality. They frequently announce in advance that they do not mean to abide by the decision of the board. Since there are no means of enforcing its award, it is the successful party before the board who has to appeal. To meet this anomaly of appeal being forced upon the successful party and to give the Conciliation Board a greater importance, it has been proposed to alter the procedure so that the loser would have to appeal. The Secretary for Labour says on this subject, in his report for 1897:

"When the whole Board of Conciliation is unanimous, that is to say, when the employers' representatives, the workers' representatives, and the chairman, all agree that certain things should be done, the board should have the same power as the higher court to make its award binding on both parties. In some cases at present, the time of members of the board is wasted because the intention of the litigants is to take the case to the Court of Arbitration under any circumstances in order that the award may have the force of law. This is an injustice to the board and a waste of public money."

Mr. Reeves told Parliament that ninety cases out of one hundred would probably be settled by the Conciliation Boards, and would not go to the Court of Arbitration. One of his supporters prophesied that the court would not be used once in twenty years.

In practical operation only one third of the cases have been settled by the Conciliation Board without an appeal to the court, but a large majority of its decisions have been sustained upon appeal; that is, in most cases, those who refused to abide by the recommendations of the

Conciliation Board, have wasted their own and their opponent's time, money, and pains by forcing an appeal to the court. This is likely to be recognised and to bring it about in time that the appeals to the court will become less frequent.

The law secures that the public gets both sides of every dispute, and gets them from the chosen representatives of each side. Public opinion is the arbitrator in such matters in the long run, and the public of New Zealand is the only one which has seen to it that it shall have the facts on which to form itself.

The government is not obliged to arbitrate with its own employés as the law now stands. As passed originally by Mr. Reeves, railroad employés, the largest and most important class, were included; but a change in the system of management from Commissioners to a Minister of Railways took them out from under the act. There is a strong demand that the government shall not continue to exempt itself from the same rule it enforces on others. This was the only change recommended by the annual conference of the Trade and Labour Councils of New Zealand, at Christchurch, in April, 1899.

CHAPTER II.

THE SHOEMAKER STICKS TO THE LAST.

It was more than a year before a case was tried under the act, but its influence was felt immediately. It had been passed in August, 1894, to go into effect in January, 1895. The first case came up in May, 1896. In the meantime, many of the trade-unions and a few associations of employers registered. Although the law had been framed by one of their friends and passed with the help of the labour members, the workingmen looked the new automobile over very carefully before accepting the invitation to ride. Their scrutiny satisfied them that, though the act was not perfect, it was a good thing. Mr. Reeves was able to announce to Parliament by September, 1895, that "sixty-one trade-unions, the pick and flower of the labour of the colony, had come in under the original act prepared to surrender their right to strike—prepared to submit their disputes to fair arbitration and conciliation. Employers, too, were being registered and more unions were registering."

He was speaking to a bill which he had submitted for some improvement in the machinery
of the Arbitration Courts.   The main argument
which he advanced to secure the support of Parliament for the amending bill shows on what
practical grounds this legislation for arbitration
had been entered upon.   He warned the members that industrial troubles of the most serious
nature were impending and likely to eventuate
within a few weeks.

"There was a reason and a grave reason why
the arbitration act should be brought into operation, and within a few weeks brought into
operation it would be."

The warning of Mr. Reeves had reference to
threatened disturbances in the shoe trade, which
had been for years in a disorganised condition.
This time, thanks to the Arbitration Act, the
outbreak which he feared was averted.

He was able to announce a few weeks later to
an interested house that there had just met in
Christchurch an important conference between
the federated boot manufacturers and the associated unions of their workmen.   The anxiety
which had been felt in regard to that conference
was now at an end.   Both parties had entered
into an agreement not to have any strike or
lockout, but to refer any disputes to arbitration.

"This was the first practical use that had been

made of the industrial Conciliation and Arbitration Act in actual differences of opinion between employers and employed, and the honourable members would no doubt share with the government the pleasure of knowing that the employment of the industrial Conciliation and Arbitration Act should have been of such a practical and friendly character."

The next year the strike thus averted came up but with features never seen before. Instead of all the manufacturers and all the employés going into a pitched industrial battle, eleven men represented all the contestants on both sides, like the champions in some Italian battle in the Middle Ages. This was the first case under the arbitration law, and the case has continued to be before the court, coming back in one shape or another through all the years since. It was a very important struggle in itself, and its career in the Arbitration Court illustrates nearly every phase of the new kind of strike New Zealand has invented, that in which justice strikes a balance.

The story of the relations of the shoe manufacturers and their men, before the Arbitration Court was established, exhibits both masters and men in the trade struggling with almost desperate energy to establish voluntary conciliation and arbitration. They tried by every private means to achieve the blessings of industrial peace, by conference, reason and consent.

They failed in this private effort because of the ugly and short-sighted obduracy of a few manufacturers. Then the new court was opened and we see the stability and prosperity which private conciliation could not give them introduced successfully and established and maintained by compulsory arbitration. We see compulsory arbitration doing just what the majority of the masters and the men tried to do, but could not because of a selfish minority.

Compulsion thus gives not only peace, but liberty—the will and the power to do right—liberty to work, liberty to contract with each other, liberty to live harmoniously, liberty to enjoy the fruits of honest capital and honest industry.

The history of their experience previous to the creation of the state tribunal, and afterwards, has been published by the trade-unions of boot makers in pamphlet form for general distribution. They gave it this publicity because they realised the unique interest it gained from the fact that they had been the first to take advantage of the new law, and because they hoped that it would serve as a guide to other unions who might find it necessary to avail themselves of this means of settling disputes.

The boot trade of New Zealand had been in continual ferment for many years, up to 1890, the year of the Maritime Strike.   The relations between manufacturers and workingmen had been relations of constant antagonism and dissatisfaction.   Suspicion, ill-feeling and a strong sense of injustice had been engendered on both sides.   Some solution of the difficulty came at last to be felt by all as a necessity.   This feeling was intensified by the shock given to every one by seeing the country go to the verge of civil war in the Maritime Strike.   One of the main causes of the friction and of the strikes which it caused had been the demand of the union that only unionists should be employed, and their insisting on "the custom of the trade" not to work with non-unionists.   The Boot Makers Union took the lead in opening the path to peace in 1891.   They pressed the manufacturers to imitate them by joining together in association in order that then by conference they might find a basis for working with mutual concessions.

The outcome of this invitation from the boot makers trade-union to the manufacturers of the colony was an acceptance and a conference which met in Wellington, the chief city of the colony.   This conference resulted in agreement. The employers and the men established local and central Boards of Arbitration and Conciliation on which members of both sides should be equally represented.   They thus initiated the same procedure which the arbitration law afterwards adopted.

"When the meeting finally closed both masters and men expressed their complete satisfaction with each other," says the history published by the trade-union, and "their trust that a new era had dawned and that hereafter the relations might be of a kindly character, the old differences healed by peace and goodwill from one to the other."

But to the surprise and dismay of their representatives—as well of the employers as of the men—after they had thus succeeded in harmonising their differences and providing means of arbitrating future differences, they were informed that a few manufacturers of one city—Auckland—a very small minority of the whole trade, would not accept the action of the conference and would not abide by the results.   The delegates of these manufacturers in the conference made no secret of the fact that they were personally desirous that their principals, the Auckland employers should join with the others, but these obstinately refused to do so, and the peremptory word was sent from Auckland that the employers there refused to be bound by any decision arrived at.   The Auckland manufacturers were not themselves a unit in this action, but, of course, this attitude on the part of a few was enough to shatter all that had been done.

What was known as the Auckland Strike, a very ugly, obstinate and expensive struggle, followed, and lasted about six months. During the progress of this strike, the representatives of the manufacturers of all the principal cities, including some in Auckland, united with representatives of all the trade-unions in the shoe industry in New Zealand, to issue a manifesto to the public. This explained the pains that had been taken by the majority of the manufacturers and all the unions to secure harmony, and the adoption of a rational method of conciliation, and how this had been defeated by the contumacy of an intractable minority of guerilla competitors.

"The late conference," they said, "brought about the establishment of good feeling between workingmen and manufacturers. The former were satisfied with the action of the latter, and they, in return, acknowledged the fair spirit in which the men considered every subject submitted for consideration. Courts of Arbitration and Conciliation were provided for, strikes almost considered an impossibility, while the future relations of the employer and employed presented a brighter aspect than has ever before existed."

"That a few manufacturers," these manufacturers and unionists concluded, "shall be able to gain a victory in a fight against reasonableness and fair play, we refuse to believe. Bad will it be for all, themselves included, if they do succeed, for once again fighting, dissatisfaction and discord will be introduced in the relation between employers and employés, and the last state probably will become worse than the first."

But "the few" manufacturers did win. Their victory, however, was as predicted dearly won. As a result of the defeat of the men and the breakup of the workers' union, and the filling of the factories by the manufacturers with non-union and boy labour, the employers, the labourers and the community suffered losses easily pointed out. Many small factories were started, and in a short time the competition became so keen that a number of manufacturers decided that it was not worth while to continue in business. The public suffered because the cost of production became greater than it would have been if the big manufactories had been going, and the class of work done became inferior. The boys who were put in place of men did not learn their trade thoroughly, and, when their apprenticeship was finished, had to accept work at a less rate than journeymen, and the men, of course, suffered, for those who continued to work had to put up with an uncertain employment and fluctuating wages.

These evils led to another conference after the strike, and an agreement was reached in 1892, which, like the one before it, provided for a general Board of Conciliation and Arbitration for the trade. This agreement kept peace for three years, until near the end of 1895, and successfully arbitrated several serious disputes.

At its expiration an attempt was made to form another, but some of the manufacturers refused to come to terms. They followed up this refusal to renew the old agreement by promulgating a new and harsh schedule of wages, rules and conditions, changing the men's position seriously for the worse. The men refused to accept these new terms.

The situation then was this, said one of the labour men who had a vigorous vocabulary, "Should the vast majority of the manufacturers and the employés and the general public who wanted arbitration and peace, stability and prosperity, lose them to enable a few cranks or crooks of competition to get the start of humaner men? The right of 'free contract,' 'managing my own business,' 'liberty,' for which this minority held out against the rest of the trade and the community, was nothing more

nor less than a right to sneak, cheat, cut and
steal away their neighbour's business and property by cruel employment and cruel competition.
The bulk of the trade could gain no advantage
from letting these men have their own way, for
many of them would be driven out of business
by the cuts in prices which cuts in wages
would make possible. The supreme law in New
Zealand, as everywhere else, is the general welfare.   There, as elsewhere, a part is not to be
allowed to make itself greater than the whole."

This crisis in the shoe trade came just at the
moment when public opinion in New Zealand,
worn out with the evils of strikes, had resolved
to find a substitute. The people were sick of
battle-field arbitration, and wanted court-room
arbitration, and what they wanted they gave
themselves, like good democrats.

The answer of New Zealand to intractable
minorities, either of trade-unions or employers,
who wanted to fight when everybody else
wanted peace, was that arbitration was the only
ethical and economical way to settle otherwise
irreconcilable disputes. The overwhelming majority of the whole people wanted it, the public
welfare and public morality agreed in demanding it, and therefore "You must arbitrate."

When the ethical convictions and the economic interests of a vast preponderance of the

community unite as to the need of a change, that change will surely come. No Anglo-Saxon community that has reached this state of mind has ever yet hesitated to pass any "compulsory law" necessary to enforce the demands of public opinion.

The compulsion, let it never be forgotten, was not that employers or workingmen must do business at "prices fixed by law and force." The compulsion was that they must settle these prices by arbitration instead of vendetta. The compulsion was to arbitrate. The arbitration being by an outsider, an impartial and competent person, would decide on prices that would be fair to all. If there must be a sacrifice, it would apportion it justly. If there was a profit, it would see that all got their share of it.

Another disastrous strike would ordinarily have followed the action of the manufacturers when the agreement of 1892 expired in 1895. But in the meantime the Compulsory Arbitration law had come into effect, and the men, with the encouragement of many of the manufacturers, sick and weary with finding themselves back where they had been, after seven years of hard work to make strikes impossible, resolved to see if the new machinery of the state could not be used to put an end to this chronic war, and give them—what they had failed to get by private effort—lasting peace.

Under the act the men could have called the manufacturers before the court whether they wanted to come or not. But, perhaps, because they thought a conciliatory tone was more becoming in appealing to a Board of Conciliation, they wrote their employers asking them if they would meet them before the board. The manufacturers assented.

The men were also entitled, under the act, to a continuance of the then rates of wages and other conditions, without change during the arbitration. But here again, they preferred to seem to receive as a favour that which they would have had now as a right. They asked the manufacturers if, pending the arbitration, the old rules and rates would remain in force. To this the manufacturers also assented cordially, as they could easily do, since they would have had no right to refuse.

The men asked for the privilege of having counsel, but the manufacturers replied that they did not intend to be so represented, and therefore must deny the request.

The proceedings before the Board of Conciliation opened with an amicable compliment from the principal representative of the manufacturers.

"First of all," he said, "I should like to compliment the employés on taking the course they have, and not going out on a strike, which would have been a deplorable thing to do. I hope we shall work harmoniously together and do the thing which is just and right."

A later remark by one of the manufacturers before the board shows how tenaciously they clung to what has always been the principal contention of the manufacturers in these disputes— their right to ignore the organisation and the representatives of their men.

"I must say at once," said this representative of the Manufacturers' Association, "on behalf of the manufacturers, that they will not for a moment negotiate with outside persons. They will not deal with irresponsible bodies, or with men not in their employ."

But this brave talk did not prevent their complying with the order of the court when it was given, that they should deal with unions of their men, whether they chose to designate them as "irresponsible bodies" or not.

The award of the Board of Conciliation was accepted by the manufacturers, but rejected by the men, and an appeal was taken to the Court of Arbitration.

It is noteworthy that the first trade to try the new tribunal was one in which a voluntary Conciliation Board had been organised by both sides, and had settled satisfactorily all disputes referred to it, and had lapsed only on account of the refusal of a few among the employers to renew the arrangement.

If the men were right in the point they made, quoted above, as to the expensiveness of the manufacturers' victory to themselves, they were, in making this appeal to the Arbitration Court, fighting the cause of the majority and the better class of the manufacturers as well as their own.

That an Arbitration Act can operate as much for the protection of employers against guerilla competitors as for the protection of labour against capital, is one of the great discoveries being made by experience in this experiment. Manufacturers in New Zealand are beginning to see this and take advantage of it.

I learned of several cases in which, by assisting their employés to organise and appeal to the Court of Arbitration, the manufacturers sought to obtain decisions which would bind not merely themselves, but also their uncontrollable competitors. Such a competitor can by this use of the Arbitration Court be prevented from making the cuts in wages which enable him to cut prices to the ruin of all who do not imitate him in squeezing out of the employés the funds to fight business rivals.

Like the strike that had preceded it, this contest with the masters before the Board of Con-

ciliation and the Arbitration Court lasted six
months, from May until November. But with
what a difference. One had stopped the factories and brought misery and distress to thousands of men, women and children. The other
took only a dozen men from their counting-
rooms and the working-bench. While they
debated, the industry went on, wages and profits
rolled in their accustomed channels into the
hands that earned them. One strike in this
trade had cost the men alone thirty thousand
dollars, and had created the angriest feelings.
But the arbitration was a quiet, almost friendly
debate, and the participants, speaking in public
and before the court, had to control their tem-
pers and their tongues.

At the close of the case, his Honour, the presiding Judge, complimented both sides on "the
thorough and clear way in which the matter
had been presented and the good feeling which
had been shown."

He requested that one representative of each
side would remain in attendance to instruct the
court, if any techincal points should arise that
needed further explanation. The Judge said
that the court hoped to be able to give a decision
on the following day, but it was a fortnight before he and his associates were ready with it.

The court laid down a rule of the greatest

interest, which has since been followed. The workingmen had asked for an award enforcing the "custom of the trade" and directing the manufacturers to employ only trade-union men. While this was refused, the court held that members of the union should be given employment in preference to non-members, provided "there are members of the union who are equally qualified with non-members to perform the particular work required to be done, and ready and willing to undertake it."

This position was taken by the court because it was found to have been the custom of the trade to employ trade-union men, and the Court of Arbitration has, throughout its career, followed the conservative policy of making its award conform as closely as possible to what is proved to be the practice.

It has, for example, in other cases, declined to give trade-unions this preference where it was shown that they had not previously achieved any such preference for themselves.

Another reason given by the court for this preference was the wording of the title of the act. This then stood as originally passed, "An act to encourage the formation of industrial unions and associations, and to facilitate the settlement of industrial disputes by conciliation and arbitration."

The court held that the title must be considered as part of the act in determining the intention of the legislature.

This policy of giving trade-unions preference wherever possible, without disturbing the settled practice of the business, has since been followed by the court, and it is one of the most important rules of action established under the arbitration law of New Zealand.

While giving members of the union precedence in employment in this case, the court required that non-union and trade-union men at work side by side should work harmoniously, under the same conditions, and receive equal pay for equal work. The employer was expressly conceded "the fullest control over the management of his factory," with full liberty "to introduce machinery without notice," with no restrictions upon out-put or the method of working.

The hours were limited to not more than nine in one day, nor more than forty-eight in a week. Extra pay for overtime was given. The number of apprentices to be employed in each department was definitely fixed. Ten dollars a week was established as the lowest rate to be paid. "The minimum wage" this is called.

Superior men were given as much more as they could earn. The rates of piece-work were fixed in proportion.

The court dealt with the question of the pay of inferior men as well as of the average workmen. There would, of course, be men who could not earn even the minimum, but whose services would still be needed by their employers. These could be given work, but their wages were to be determined, if any question arose, by the Board of Conciliation.

To prevent sweating, it was required that all work should be done in the shops.

The trade custom of Boards of Conciliation and Arbitration within the trade itself, for which the better class of manufacturers and the workingmen had so bravely contended, was restored, and a full and exact constitution for these boards was laid down, and they were given, within the trade, the powers of fixing prices, determining conditions and settling disputes, which the Court of Arbitration itself possesses for all industries. This power to create trade tribunals of conciliation and arbitration is one of the most important functions of the New Zealand Court of Arbitration.

This settlement was achieved with average justice to all concerned because, for one reason, the parties to the dispute had had to make public all the conditions of their industry, and to have them attested by witnesses and experts, handled in the ways usual in courts.

This ability of each side in the Arbitration

Court to subject the claims made by the other to the fullest examination was in striking contrast to their helplessness previously.

One of the most interesting pages of the history of the boot trade dispute published by the trade-union, is that in which it recites, and answers as it can, the assertions made by the Auckland manufacturers who refused in 1891 to be bound by the results of the conference. These assertions when made had been met in the manifesto of the employers and the workingmen simply by counter-assertions, for this was the best that they could do in the days when there was not yet compulsory publicity.

The Auckland manufacturers, for instance, had asserted that living was cheaper in their town than elsewhere, and that the men were equally well off with smaller wages than elsewhere. To this the manifesto had to content itself with replying: "No proof has been given, and probably the difference, if any, is infinitesimal." But when statements like this were made before the Court of Arbitration proof had to be brought. The Auckland manufacturers had to back up their assertions with actual facts and figures subject to all the sifting and testing processes of court procedure.

Another claim which the Auckland men had made was that they bought their materials cheaper, and hence charged less for their goods, and another, that the wages their men earned at present were large enough. To all these statements their opponents could make no adequate reply when there was no Arbitration Court or Conciliation Board; but when these were once in operation, no assertion of that sort could avail the manufacturers who made it unless they were prepared to substantiate it with indisputable evidence, which could stand cross-examination and pass muster with experts and judges trained to deal with all kinds of mystification, statistical and otherwise.

Statements like these were made before the Arbitration Court, but now they were investigated by the representatives of labour and capital. All the necessary books had to be produced, experts were called in, and questions of fact were all disposed of in a way which made it impossible to doubt that the truth had been ascertained.

The court had the power to make its decision binding on the trade for two years, but it thought it was wiser, as it was the first decision, to let it run for only one year.

At the end of the year, the dispute broke out afresh. The two associations of masters and men had a meeting and agreed that it was of no use to go before the Board of Conciliation, for neither side would rest until it had, first, exhausted its last chance of getting what it wanted by going to the court of last resort, and second, had got a decision which it knew it had to obey, whether it wanted to or not.

In other words, both sides wanted compulsion, not conciliation!

The employers, as the remark quoted by one of their number at the beginning of the conciliation had foreshadowed, made their principal stand against that part of the decision which gave preference to trade-unions.   There were other points at issue, but the main fight was on this.

The men wanted forty-four hours a week; the manufacturers were willing to continue forty-eight hours a week, and the court held with them.

The manufacturers agreed to the average wage of ten dollars a week.   The workingmen were denied some increases of pay they asked for instructors' apprentices and for skilled men to put at work on machines, but they were given increased rates for piece-work.   Some of their demands as to the limitation of the number of apprentices were conceded, others refused.

The employers made no opposition to the provision, designed to put an end to sweating, that all work should be done in the factory.

Both sides agreed that new machinery could be introduced at will by the employer.

The sore point with the manufacturers was that they were forbidden to employ non-union men until they had given places to all the union men who were competent and willing to do the work. This was threshed out again as it had been at the first hearing. The manufacturers were resolved that, as they had said, they would not deal with "irresponsible bodies," nor negotiate with "outside persons," meaning delegates of the trade-unions.

The Boot Makers demanded that—

"Employers shall employ members of the New Zealand Federated Boot Makers Union in preference to non-members, provided there are members of the union who are equally qualified with non-members to perform the particular work required to be done, and are ready and willing to undertake it."

The Employers, that—

"Employers shall not discriminate between members of the New Zealand Boot Trade Union and non-members."

The court made its decision in the exact language of the employés. This time it made its award binding for two years, the full limit allowed, until September 1, 1900.

For six years then, from September, 1895, until September, 1900, the manufacturers and the men in the boot trade will have been enabled, notwithstanding many serious differences, many of them still existing, to go on working. For six years they will have had no strikes, no lockouts; there will have been no unexpected demands by the men, no sudden cuts by the masters. These six years have been years of constant dispute, but there has not been one day's idleness, not one day of passion, not one blow struck. Both sides are still contending, but they continue at work and are prosperous.

When the two years' period expires in 1900, the same peaceful means of settlement will be at the disposal of both sides, and both will no doubt, as they have already done, decline conciliation and choose compulsory arbitration because it is compulsory, and guarantees finality and certainty and equal conditions for all.

Very likely, however, by that time the two parties in this trade will do as others have done under the new régime, they will agree to go on according to the terms fixed by the court without troubling it again. Or, they may follow still a different course, as has also occurred in

another trade.   They may ask the president of
the court to meet with them informally, and,
after an amicable conversation, make a voluntary agreement along the lines suggested by
him.

Is not this a civilised way for civilised people
to settle their differences?   If there is a better,
where is it to be found?   In such wholesale disaster as that of the strike in the quarries of Lord
Penrhyn, or at Homestead, or in the complete
paralysis that for months last year held almost
all the industries of Denmark in its grasp?

The representatives of the boot manufacturers' associations pleaded almost piteously before
the court that they would be ruined if it granted
the demands of the men.   The court, these representatives pleaded, could bind their association, but "it had no power to bind outside boot
factories, and this would give those outside the
association unfair advantages, as they would be
quite unrestricted as to wages and conditions
under which they, as employers, should work.
This would cripple the others who belonged to
the association."

The court dignifiedly allowed this limiting
construction of its powers to pass uncorrected.
But an opportunity soon came to show whether
it had power to bind outside manufacturers, and
would have the courage to use it.

There were three men not in the manufacturers' association, employers of non-union men,
and they disregarded the award which had been
made against those inside the association.   The
workingmen of the union at once summoned
them before the court.   They were able to do
this because the act is purposely so framed that
workmen can proceed as well against individual
employers as against associations of them.   The
court decided that these manufacturers must
adhere to the same wages and other conditions
as those which it had fixed for members of the
manufacturers' association.   But—and this is an
illustration of the practical and conservative
temper in which the judges have always administered the act—the requirement that trade-union
men must be given preference was waived.

Throughout its decisions, the court has
shown that its aim was to preserve as nearly as
possible the conditions in which it found the
trade.   It has constantly endeavoured to avoid
becoming a disturbing element in business, or
a legislator of new conditions.

Preference in this case was waived for the
reason that these outside manufacturers represented a branch of the industry in which the
men were as yet hardly organised.   The court
therefore only stipulated that there should be no
discrimination against the trade-unionists, and

required the outside manufacturers to keep all the other conditions imposed upon their competitors.

When the first award against the boot manufacturers' association expired, in December, 1897, these outsiders were, of course, also released, and they at once resumed their former attitude of free lances. The decision already described regulating the trade until September, 1900, was, as the previous one had been, also disregarded by these outsiders.

Again the trade-union called them before the court, and this time they were sharply handled there. The trade had by this time got into a condition which, in the opinion of the judges, made the preference to trade-unionists advisable, and they did not repeat their former indulgence of waiving it in behalf of these manufacturers who did not wish to join the manufacturers' association, or to carry on their business by the same methods their competitors were compelled to observe.

The presiding judge said that the conditions of the boot trade had been exhaustively dealt with by the court, and it had rendered decisions which it had meant should settle matters for the whole colony. Employers who sought to carry on their business on conditions other than those governing the trade generally, would have to show good cause why they should be allowed to do so.

The court then called upon these would-be free lances to show why they should not be bound by the award. It did not trouble the trade-union to make any statement on its side. The defendants pleaded that they had "conscientious scruples about belonging to the masters' association," and they also said they had a perfect right to employ workingmen who, like themselves, had scruples about joining a union.

His Honour said the court had nothing to do with such scruples. It would not be in violation of "conscience" for them to abide by the rules which applied to their competitors in the same business.

These manufacturers obstinately contended that they were not bound to join the masters' association. The judge said that there was no desire to force them to do so, but they must come under the same conditions as their competitors. All the employers had contended before the court, he said, that they should have liberty to employ whom they chose, but the court had decided differently. The court could, if it thought it wise, vary its decision, but, if it should do so in this case, it would be to the advantage of these three firms as against their competitors, and the court could not see its way to give them any such advantage.

After a consultation by the members of the court, its decision was announced by his Honour.

It would be grossly unfair, he said, to their competitors, if these men were exempted from the award, and the court could see no reason for exempting them.   The court therefore made an award binding these manufacturers to the same terms as the rest of the trade.

A parting shot was fired by one of the defendants who said that "whatever it cost them, the firm would not sign an industrial agreement; they had conscientious scruples."   To which the court blandly replied that, whether they had conscientious scruples or not, or signed or not, they would have to comply with the terms of the decree.

The Mohammedans have a saying that one hour of justice is worth seventy years of prayer, and in the study of so novel and important a matter as compulsory arbitration, one hour of practical experience is worth seventy years of theory.

In this instance, we see the first case which appears before the court continuing to appear before it, and we know that it will reappear. The masters and the men are both strongly organised; they hold unshakable convictions; they even have "conscientious scruples"; they are not satisfied, for neither has secured what he asked for, but they find it less intolerable to obey the award and go on than to give up the business. The trade is kept in continual agitation for six years, but how innocent the agitation! Instead of strikes, riots, starvation, bankruptcy, passion, and all the other accompaniments of the Homestead method, there has been—debate! The total loss is a few weeks' time of only a dozen men. The manufacturers have not been ruined; they have not had to shut down their works; they have not fled the country. The workingmen have gone on working, buying land and building homes and paying for them, rearing children, and building up industry and the state as well as their homes.

CHAPTER III.

"BETTER COMMITTEES THAN MOBS."

ONE of the great sayings of Kant was that we should "organise the world." The compulsory arbitration of New Zealand organises its industrial world. Its corner-stone is its invitation to labourers and capitalists to unite within themselves that they may be united with each other. One continually sees paragraphs like this in the newspapers of New Zealand:

"The iron workers of Auckland have unanimously agreed to form a union under the Conciliation and Arbitration Act, to be called The Federated Iron Workers Union. The union will embrace the boiler-makers, farriers and general smiths."

And often, though less frequently, one sees similar items announcing the organisation of the employers. At the last accounts there had been one hundred and forty trade-unions and unions of employers formed to take advantage of the Compulsory Arbitration law.   More are coming into line.

Compulsory arbitration proceeds on the teaching of experience that in labour troubles it is better to have committees than mobs to deal with, even mobs of one.   Of all mobs there have never been any more dangerous than an individual beside himself with passion and greed, defying all laws of God and man that he may have his own way.

Everything that can be done by the New Zealand law to encourage these organisations is done.   Manufacturers stay outside the organisation of their associates in the hope of escaping arbitration, only to find themselves as easily brought before the bar as the others.   Organisations of workingmen which are not registered under this law cannot hold land for their collective purposes and cannot sue defaulting members.   Of course they cannot vote for members of the Boards of Conciliation and Courts of Arbitration, and yet, when any disturbance arises in their trade, they find themselves brought before these boards and put under the same terms of employment as their fellows who have registered.   These are powerful inducements for organisation and registration both by employers and workingmen, and there are others.

There is not a detail of any grievance a work-

ingman may have which cannot be brought out
before the arbitrators and the public if he is a
member of a registered trade-union. For workingmen so organised there is no more "refusal
to receive committees," no more insistence upon
"dealing with individuals," no more talk from
the co-working capitalists to them of "my business."

When the member of the registered trade-
union asks to be given some of the profits, there
is no more putting him off with sweeping statements that, "The business would not stand any
increase in wages;" statements which elsewhere
have to be accepted because there are no means
of either challenging them or verifying them.

Loose allegations of that kind are not safe
before the Court of Arbitration, for it can compel the production of books and papers and the
attendance of witnesses to make them good.
Public opinion in a dispute where a registered
union of labour or capital is concerned, does not
have to get its information from one-sided
newspaper accounts of the grievances of either
employers or employés.

From the first, through all its decisions, the
Arbitration Court has given trade-unionists,
wherever possible, the right to be employed until
they have all obtained work, before it permits
the employment of non-unionists. Various rea-

sons have at different times been given by the court to sustain this policy.   Besides the reasons already mentioned, found in the wording of the title of the law and in the custom of the trade, the courts have held that "the advantages which were procured by unions for their members were obtained at some expense, and therefore it was but right, provided entrance to the union was not prohibited, that preference should be given to unionists, and if non-unionists would not pay the small fee and contributions to entitle them to the advantages, they had nothing to complain of."

In the iron moulders case the court expressed the opinion that both masters and men benefited by the existence of the unions; that it was better for all parties to deal with bodies than with individuals.

It is a curious phenomenon of antipodal public opinion that America is being swept by waves of opposition on one side of society to trade-unions and of opposition on the other side to unions of capitalists, while in New Zealand the people and the government favour the fullest organisation of both.

The first judge of the Arbitration Court, though a man of the highest character and unquestioned impartiality, still was so thoroughly identified socially with those who are not expected to have much sympathy with the working classes, that the trade-unionists felt no little apprehension as to what was to be expected of his interpretation of the law. But it was he who initiated this policy of preference, and established it so firmly that it has never been departed from. Though he was, in fact, what some called a "Tory" judge, and was feared correspondingly by workingmen, he decided nine times out of ten in favour of the men; not, he said, because they were workingmen, but because they had the right of the case.

But, though the Court of Arbitration gives a preference to trade-unionists when it thinks that that is called for, it does not hesitate to withhold it when the circumstances seem to make that the proper course to pursue.

In a dispute between a number of gold mining companies whose employés were not well organised, the court only directed that "each of the companies shall not discriminate against members of the union, and shall not, either directly or indirectly, do anything with a view to injuring the union."

And upon trade-unionists it laid the injunction, "Members of the union shall work in harmony with non-union men."

In another case where the Court of Arbitration did not find itself called upon to give the preference in employment to trade-unionists, it still recommended that the steamship owners before the court should allow union officials to go on board their vessels and consult with seamen at reasonable times. But the court stated that it did not intend that its recommendation should have the force of law, as the court did not consider that it had power to give a person liberty to enter upon a steamship or other property against the will of the owner.

In another case, the court allowed the company the option of employing non-union men, but specified that there was to be no preference in their favour.

In a case before the Conciliation Board involving the Bakers Union of Dunedin, the chairman of the board said that the ruling of the Arbitration Court was understood to be that, except under special circumstances, union men shall get preference of employment. This shows it to be the practice of the court to throw the burden upon the employer of bringing forward evidence to prove that in his case there were "special circumstances" militating against such a preference.

The act and its administration by the court fortifies the position of trade-unionists by allowing them to bring non-unionists in their trade before the court. They can summon the employers of these non-unionists, and by putting them under the same conditions as other employers of trade-unionists, protect themselves from being under-cut by their unorganised associates.

Employers cannot escape the obligation to employ union men on union terms by discharging their union hands and replacing them by non-unionists, for the court has decided that in such cases it still has jurisdiction.

This is one of the features of the act which has won the most favour with all sides, most of all with employers, for it prevents them from being ruined by the competitor who cuts wages in order to cut prices.

Though giving a preference to unionists, the court is careful to protect non-unionists who are at work.   Such a sentence as this occurs frequently in the decisions of the court:

"This is not to interfere with the existing engagements of non-members, whose present employers may retain them in the same or other positions."

No one can read the decisions of the court and detect the slightest trace of anything like bias for or against either labour or capital.

The court has taken some severe "falls" out of trade-unions which have asked for preference of employment for their members.

In a case between the Wellington Seamen's

Union and the shipowners, the judge entirely
refused to make the ruling which was asked by
the seamen, that they should have the preference
in employment. The judge pointed out that the
union did not dispute the fact that the shipowners had faithfully abided by the previous
ruling of the court that they should not in any
way interfere with union men as such, or with
the unions. That in itself, he said, was a very
strong reason why matters should be left as they
were, but he pointed out that there were other
reasons to be taken into account.

The management and navigation of ships, he
said, stand, in many respects, on quite a different footing from the management of factories
or other ordinary businesses. Above all things,
it is necessary to have discipline on shipboard.
Those who follow a seafaring life must, to a
certain extent, recognise that, like soldiers and
men-of-war's-men, they must give up their
rights of individual action for the public benefit.
Every order given by an officer must be unhesi-
tatingly obeyed, whether reasonable or unreasonable, otherwise the lives and property of the
public would be in danger.

One of the facts in this case which had been
brought out was that the company before the
court was on friendly terms with the seamen's
union of another city, Dunedin, and to compel a

shipowner whose vessel plied between these two ports to give preference to the Wellington seamen, the court pointed out might cause very unpleasant and even dangerous complications.

Had a strong case been made out, he said, he might have had to try to get over it, but no such case has been made out. It had been urged that, if this union did not secure preference for its members, some of them, who were individually selfish, might leave it, thinking they were not getting the value for their money.

But the court held that that was no reason whatever for giving a preference, and added his hope and belief that members of the union would be more manly, more far-seeing than they had been described to be in the presentation of this argument.

This award gave the seamen a few concessions and fixed the conditions of employment for both sides until August, 1901.

Another case in which a trade-union asking preference was handled severely by the court, was that of the engineers of Christchurch, and it is worth giving in some detail, as it brings into clear view some interesting aspects of the operation of compulsory arbitration, and illustrates vividly the ability of judges, "who know nothing of business," to see the practical points of a complicated matter.

The court refused the engineers of Christchurch preference in employment, and emphasised its refusal by the unusual course of adding to its award a special memorandum, giving its reasons at great length to the trade and the public.

It almost seems as if the court desired to make it conspicuous that it had no leanings toward the side of labour, though it was so frequently deciding in its favour against capital.

How far is this union, the court asked, "really representative of the great body of men employed in the trade affected?"

Its analysis of the figures of membership showed that "the union demand is the demand of seventeen or eighteen men out of one hundred and fifty-one, to enforce their views upon the whole body."

The number of men indirectly concerned was very large, not less than one thousand six hundred and thirty, according to the government returns. The court declared that because it was so small a minority, and for other reasons which it gave, it was compelled to the conclusion that the demand of the union was inimical to the interests of the majority of the workingmen.

Other claims made by the union were handled with equal severity. They asked that the hours be limited to forty-four a week. This was refused, as there was no evidence that such a change was wanted by any considerable number of the men.

The union asked that the maximum rates of wages which skilled workingmen were earning be made "the minimum wage," or the wage of the average worker. The effect of this would be, the judge said, "to throw out of employment a large body of steady and deserving men who are not sufficiently skilled to command the highest wage." The court said:

"It was not disputed on the part of the union that, if the advance demanded were conceded, numbers of men who were now earning a decent livelihood must necessarily quit their present employment, and the only answer to the question as to what was to become of such men was a suggestion that they should go 'bushwhacking,' a suggestion which appears to me to imply not only very imperfect knowledge as to what was involved in bushwhacking, but a very imperfect conception of the rights of fellow-workmen."

Another reason for not granting these and other claims was that the employers would be forced to raise the prices of their goods, such as agricultural machinery, and this they could not afford to do for "they were working in competition not only with each other, but with other similar establishments in other centres in the colony, and not only with these but also in competition with importers.   The concession of these demands would result in the speedy extinction of the agricultural implement manufacturing trade."

The Court of Arbitration has often limited the number of apprentices at the request of the unions, but in this case it would not do so.

"The main grounds," the court said, "urged in support of this claim are, first, that the trade will become over-manned unless the number of apprentices is limited; and, second, that the apprentices are not so well taught if their number exceed those suggested."

But in reply to this the court pointed out that, "up to the present time, though the number of apprentices has not been limited, the trade has not become over-manned.   The reason is that engineers are required in many other walks of life besides engineer shops, such as marine engineers, refrigerating engineers, both at sea and on shore, etc.   Engineers are also required in all large factories where machinery is used. The engineering shops are necessarily the training grounds for all these engineers, and the result has been that all the lads who have served their apprenticeship in Christchurch and have learned their trade, have had no difficulty in finding employment."

The second point, that apprentices are not well taught, if there is a large number of them, the court found to fail equally with the other.

"It has been proved beyond a doubt," it said, "that engineers trained in Christchurch shops have been able to hold their own with engineers trained in Great Britain and elsewhere, and that many of them have done remarkably well."

"It would require very special grounds, in my opinion," continued the judge, "to justify an award which would have the effect of closing the door to an employment which has so many outlets, and which is justly popular with the youth of the colony."

He then went on to point out a special ground why a claim to limit the number of engineering apprentices should be more closely scrutinised in Christchurch than elsewhere in the colony.

"There is, it seems, in Christchurch a school of engineering attended by some ninety students, all of whom require to have a practical knowledge of their trade, and this they can only acquire in the engineering shops in Christchurch. It is not contested that this school does good work, and that it is a highly desirable institution, yet the result of conceding the union demand in the matter would be to debar many of the students from acquiring the practical knowledge which is essential to them."

In the truly practical spirit of our Anglo-Saxon law, the judge took special pains to show that in this ruling he was considering only the actual and special circumstances of the case before him, and was not establishing precedents which could be indiscriminately applied.

"I desire to guard myself," he said, "from seeming to lay down any rules as to when it may be proper to give such a privilege to the members of the union, because I think that each case must stand upon its own merits, and the claim must in every case be carefully scrutinised."

The Honourable John Rigg, one of the representatives of labour in the Upper House of the New Zealand Parliament, in discussing this decision, said:

"Those, I consider, are very good grounds for the decision, and we see here the absolute impartiality with which the disputes have been determined."

This decision indicated no change of heart in the Court of Arbitration and no apostasy to its principle, as to the importance of trade-unions nor their rights to a preference of employment when the circumstances called for it.

The court continued after this decision as before to give preference to trade-unions. This was awarded in fact by the Board of Conciliation and the Court of Arbitration to all the trade-unions in the same town of Christchurch, in all the disputes which have come up since, and there have been a number of them—the printers, bakers, butchers, cooks, tinsmiths, sheet-iron workers, tailors, grocers, furniture makers.

How far the court was from any bias against trade-unionism is shown in the case of a coal-mining company which had discharged three men because they were members of an industrial union—the president, the secretary, and the son of the secretary. Their union called the company to account and the case was heard by the Court of Arbitration. The court awarded that the company should pay by way of damages to the union $283, which was the wages the men had lost, and should also pay the costs, amounting to $57.

The court ordered the reinstatement of the men discharged for their unionism:

"The employers, if so requested by any of them (the discharged men) within one week from the making of this award, shall take them into their service in the same capacities they occupied at the time of their dismissal."

The Arbitration Court has gone so far as to

recommend men who were not organised to form unions.

Some range-makers wanted to be included in an award in a dispute affecting some tinsmiths and sheet-metal workers. In giving his decision, the judge said that the court had come to the conclusion that the range-makers could not come under the award. But at the same time, he continued, there was no reason why these men should not form a union of their own, and then, if they had a grievance they could apply to the court to fix their wages.

Women workers were intended by Mr. Reeves and Parliament to be given all the benefits of the act, but they did not seem to consider themselves covered by its language. The act said "workmen," and the new spirit of independence which marks the sex in our century, apparently prompted them to ignore the act because it did not specially mention them.

To meet this difficulty it was necessary to amend the bill the year after its passage. In offering this amendment, the Minister of Labour, Mr. Reeves, said that it had been found impossible to persuade the women that "workmen" included work-women. They were under the impression that they were debarred from registering under the act because of the exclusive use of this masculine word. He therefore

proposed to substitute for "workmen" the word
"workers." With this concession to the dignity
of their sex, the women workers have since
registered freely, and have obtained important
advantages, but especially in the clothing trade
as will be shown.

"There is much virtue," says Shakespeare, "in
your 'if.'" There is much virtue in New Zealand in "workman." This word is legally de-
fined in the land regulations of the colony as
meaning any man or woman over twenty-one,
"who is engaged in any form of manual, cleri-
cal or other work for hire or reward," and is not
worth more than $750.

This word is a straw which would suggest
at once to any one knowing the New Zealand
character, that others than those ordinarily
known as artisans or manual workers would be
likely to claim for themselves from the Arbitration Law the benefits of what it gives.

This has been the case.

In my morning paper at Christchurch, I read
one day:

"The employés in the grocery trade have recently formed an industrial union, and during
the past fortnight have submitted certain conditions to the employers. As, however, the
great body of them simply ignore the requests
of the union, some forty employers have been

incited to appear before the Board of Conciliation of Thursday next, at 2 P. M."

All classes of employés in the groceries had joined in the organisation—clerks, bookkeepers, order collectors, head draymen and other draymen.

The decision of the Conciliation Board was in favour of the men on almost all points.   The board recommended that the minimum or average wage for these men should be £2 5s. ($11.25) a week.   It provided that those who were unable to earn the minimum could be still employed at lesser wages to be approved, if necessary, by the Conciliation Board.

The award provided for extra pay for overtime at the rate of one shilling (twenty-five cents) an hour, and all time worked on holidays was to be classed as overtime.

The award also gave the members of the Canterbury Grocers' Union "preference of employment over non-members," with the usual stipulation, "provided that the members of the union are equally qualified with non-members to perform the particular work required to be done, and are ready and willing to undertake it."

The employers were required to give the secretary of the union twenty-four hours' notice when they wanted additional clerks before they were allowed to engage any non-union men.

But the representative of the employers when this award was made announced that the grocers would not accept it, and would compel their men to appeal to the Arbitration Court. There the point would be pressed by the employers that the grocery trade was not an "industry," and the clerks' union could not therefore be registered under the Arbitration Act. In this position the employers claimed they were fortified by the best legal advice obtainable.

They had made this point before the Board of Conciliation, but the board was unanimous in its opinion that the clerks were properly before the court, and that the case must proceed. If the action of the Board of Conciliation had been sustained by the appeal, and the objections of the employers overruled, other clerks and employés of mercantile houses, and even of financial concerns, would have organised and claimed the protection of the act, for their wages and terms of employment. The Arbitration Court, however, reversed the decision of the Board of Conciliation, and held that an issue between the grocers and their assistants was not an "industrial dispute" within the meaning of the act. But it suggested that the union could ask the Supreme Court for a mandamus to the Arbitration Court to hear the case.

One of the leading papers of Christchurch

in discussing this case said that, if the Arbitration Court did not sustain the right of the grocery clerks to take advantage of the act, the legislature would certainly amend it in their favour.   In one way or the other, either by an interpretation by the Court of Arbitration which will admit clerks, etc., or by amendment of the law, we may look to see drug clerks, grocery employés, in fact, all employés, including, very likely, domestic workers in the family and farm labourers, invited to enlist in the army of non-combatants.   They are all workmen in the sense which has been given that word officially by the New Zealand government in its land legislation.

Public policy will see the same reasons for this universal inclusion of all men and women who receive hire as for the inclusion of one class.   The Compulsory Arbitration law will then become a truly democratic measure, giving its helping hand to all.

It took a year for the grocers' assistants to get their case decided.   This delay reveals one of the practical defects of the operation of the law.   The President of the Arbitration Court having other courts to sit in is slow in getting around the colony, and there was consequently for many months no session of the court in Christchurch.   The awards of the Conciliation Board not being enforceable, its award in their favour had for that length of time been of no practical value to the clerks. The government has promised to remedy this difficulty by increasing the judicial force of the Arbitration Court.

By its advance to include women as well as men, we see the New Zealand Arbitration Law grounding itself more firmly, step by step, in the life of the people, aggrandising itself as a good institution will do, constantly gaining a larger place and binding the citizens to itself more and more. During these six years of existence it has grown every day more important.

There is no right without its duty. With this preference of employment which it gives trade-unionists, the Court of Arbitration lays upon them corresponding obligations. A paragraph in the decision in favour of preference for employment for the painters of Christchurch shows this.

"The union," the court says, "is to keep in a convenient place, within one mile from the chief post-office in Christchurch, a book of trade-unionists out of employment, together with their qualifications—a note to be made when any of the workmen obtain employment. The executive of the union is to use their best endeavours to verify all entries, and shall be answerable as for a breach of this award in case any entry therein shall be wilfully false of their knowledge, or in case they shall not have used reasonable endeavours to verify the same. The book is to be open between 8 A. M. and 5 P. M. to all employers. In case of the failure of the union accurately to keep such book, the employers shall be at liberty to employ other than members of the union. Notice by advertisement in the Christchurch morning papers is to be given of the place where such book is to be kept."

Another thing the court demands of the trade-unions in return for this preference of employment given them, is that they shall not be monopolies; they must be inclusive not exclusive.

In a case brought by some iron moulders, the judge, in granting the union preference in employment, said that, at the same time it was opposed to granting anything which tended to make the union a close corporation. The court had, therefore, closely examined the rules of the union to see whether there was any provision against the admission of men of sober habits and good character, and it added the stipulation that before the trade-unions could be given a preference for their members, they must not prohibit the admission of such men.

One reason for the very severe treatment given the Christchurch engineers already spoken of, was that the judge found that there were a large number of men employed in the district who were "not only debarred from becoming members of the union under its rules, but would, under the scheme proposed by the union, be debarred from working in the trades in which they are at present employed."

"Unions which sought this advantage," the judge intimated, "must be practically open to every person employed in the trade who desires to join."

This ruling of the court is in line with the general policy of the trade-unions, which, unlike other monopolies, usually do their best to increase the number of monopolists. But this court has made it easier for trade-unionists in New Zealand to live up to it than elsewhere by the establishment of the "minimum wage."

In every dispute the court fixes this minimum or average wage. Its decisions carefully provide for superior, average, and inferior men. No one can be employed for less than the average, except, as has been already explained, men not competent to earn the average, and the rate paid them must, if questioned, be sanctioned by the local Board of Conciliation.

It is no matter to the trade-union, then, how many members it admits; there is no danger that the overcrowding will lead to lower wages, for the wages cannot be lowered.

The object of the Arbitration law was to

prevent strikes. These rulings of the Court of Arbitration make the institution also a powerful instrument in the mitigation of competition between workingmen, and in the maintenance of higher wages and a better standard of life.

On the other side the law ameliorates competition among the capitalists by preventing them from cutting wages in order to cut prices.

Not being allowed counsel in the Arbitration Court puts the workingmen on their mettle and will have a mighty educational influence upon them. As the visitor sees the presiding judge disciplining the representatives of the employers and the men, he realises that this court is a school for "grown-ups." The judge, despite himself, cannot sometimes help showing an irritation which obviously has need of all the consolation he can get from the reflection that his school is, perhaps, the most important one in the world.

In one of the cases I attended, the judge had frequent occasion to caution the representative of a union on his conduct of the evidence, and to advise him as to what he should not do. Finally, his Honour, in a state bordering on despair, exclaimed :

"It appears to me that so far as the proceedings of this court are concerned, the legal profession will have to be admitted. You," he said, to the union's advocate, "are not conducting the proceedings in an intelligible manner, and all I can get is inference."

The educational influence of the court extends to other matters than the modes of arguing the case and handling evidence.

At a meeting of the Arbitration Court when a witness was being examined as to his average earnings, his Honour said it was the duty of all trade-unionists to keep a proper account. If they did not want to do this for themselves, they should do it in the interests of their union and their associates.

And on the same day an employer called by the association of master-painters, in giving his evidence about wages and other matters, frequently used the phrase "I think." The judge interrupted him to say that an employer keeping books should "know," not "think," and that in such matters as these, he could take suppositions only for what they were worth.

Mr. Reeves, in first presenting his bill, laid stress on the great service that would be rendered the community in the simple fact that it would keep industrial disputes free from passion.

An instance of this occurred on the first day of the session of the court at which I was present at Christchurch.

One of the advocates was putting questions

in a style which certainly could not be considered polite, but which there would have been none to repress in an old-time conference between masters and men.   He was corrected by the judge, who said:

"I cannot allow insulting language or insulting questions to be used in this court.   The proceedings must be conducted with the same decorum as if I were in the Supreme Court, and any one acting to the contrary will be excluded from participating in the proceedings."

In the presence of the presiding judge, a person so important as the Judge of the Supreme Court, and a man who holds their destiny in his hands, the contestants must behave themselves. Every student of his own and other people's human nature knows how steadying a part it plays in keeping his temper, to be obliged to look and act as if he were keeping it.

Discussions between workingmen and their employers, carried on without such restraining influences as are found in the Arbitration Court, often ripen into most devastating disputes from the mere license given to an angry tongue.

The point has been made that the arbitration act as administered gives an unfair advantage to the trade-unionists, and that this advantage goes to a very small minority, since only a slight proportion of the workingmen in New Zealand, as in Great Britain and the United States, are

organised. Even in Great Britain, the home
of trade-unionism, only about one sixth of the
men are enrolled.

To this extent the act does accentuate an inequality. But as any seven men can form a
union in the trade, they need not endure this
discrimination a day longer than they themselves wish to.

The only circumstances which would make it
possible that any industrial dispute in New Zealand should escape arbitration, would be the
entire absence of any organisation, either
among the masters or the men.

If such a thing were conceivable as an agreement between the employers and the men not to
invoke the courts, but to go on striking and
locking out at their own sweet will, and should
agree for that purpose to refrain on both sides
from organisation, we should certainly have a
case, but the only case in which there could be
no arbitration.

The state has no independent power of its
own to investigate labour troubles, nor to move
to settle them of its own motion.

The Minister of Labour, Mr. Reeves, in
offering his bill, declared himself to be in favour
of such initiative, but thought that the community was not yet ripe to entrust the government
with such power.

The New Zealand law is so far altogether

individualistic.   Persons can compel arbitration, but the people cannot.   The protection of the public interests is for the present then entrusted to the initiative of the aggrieved individual, under the certainty that the class feeling between labour and capital is strong enough to insure action.   Trusts like those now coming into favour in England, such as that of the bedstead makers of Birmingham, in which the masters and the men have united to fleece the public, would not be very promising subjects for compulsory arbitration.

The organisation of capital and labour both could have no greater stimulant than compulsory arbitration, and for the trade-unions it has this special attraction: Beyond the collective workingman we can see the collective capitalist in the trade-unions saving the funds they now waste in strikes for making contracts on their own account, and for co-operative production, house building, land owning and banking.

By a late decision, January, 1900, the court rules that if preference of employment is given trade-unionists they, on their side, must prefer employers who are organised in associations rather than outsiders.   The rule must work both ways.   If organised labour asks preference, it must accord organised capital the same advantage.

CHAPTER IV.

A NEW SONG OF THE SHIRT.

In replying to a gibe from the London Times, "that the act does not inspire others with the satisfaction with which it is contemplated by its author," Mr. Reeves wrote, in 1898:

"As for my 'satisfaction,' I am happy that the act has got to work and has done good service during three years of use; especially am I glad that it has helped the women workers."

There is no chapter of the operation of this new institution which has a more fascinating social interest than that which tells how it has helped the sewing women of New Zealand out of the sweatshops, and, quite as important, how it keeps them out.

The clothing trade in all countries is a hatchery for the foulest evils that haunt modern industry. Its workers are largely women and children, the most helpless of all.   Many of them, supported at home, seek the occupation to get a little something to add to the family resources, and for pin money.   They drag down the wages—the cost of production—of those who must live on what they make.

No labour struggles are more deeply distressing to the public than the convulsive efforts which are made every now and then, so ineffectually, by the working girls and working women of these trades, to escape from their starvation wages and degrading conditions of employment.

The conscience of the New Zealand public was swept about ten years ago by one of those waves of feeling which periodically arouses our people as well to a feverish interest and spasmodic attempts to find a remedy.

At both ends of the colony, in Auckland and Wellington in the north, and in Dunedin and other cities in the south, the workers, aided by clergymen and other well-known citizens, and the newspapers, began to stir to put an end to what was felt to be as much a danger as a scandal.

In Dunedin, the agitation began with the shirt-makers who were miserably sweated. "Dunedin," as one of its senators said to me in describing this movement, "is a small town. Everybody knows everybody else.   It was well-

known that the manufacturers had reduced
wages below the living point.   It had become a
public scandal.   There was no difficulty in getting the parsons and the newspaper men to take
up the crusade against the sweatshops.   The
newspapers and the clergymen took the lead."

Now, Miss Whitehorn, the Secretary of the
Tailoresses Union, assured me, "Practically all
the Dunedin tailoresses are organised."

In this work, she said, "The shirt-makers and
the other working women had been assisted by
almost all of the employers—all but six or seven
—who helped them to organise.

"One of the most important uses of the Compulsory Arbitration Law, these manufacturers
are finding," she continued, "is to give inducements to the workers to organise, and to bring the
minority of the masters into line.   It is used in
such cases not against the employers as a whole,
but against those of them who are irreconcilable.   The majority of the manufacturers as
well as the master tailors, those who run factories and those who have shops, favoured the
organisation of their employés into trade-
unions, and even allowed the walking delegates
of the union to visit the shops and persuade the
workers to join the unions.

"The shirt-makers and other factory clothing
workers of the principal towns in the South Isl-

and, Dunedin, Christchurch and Wellington, are, in consequence of this movement and the help of their employers, now working by a 'log' —a schedule of prices and conditions arranged at a voluntary conference in Wellington, in November, 1897, to run a year, afterwards renewed for six months.

"The employers met us in this conference in the best spirit.   They could not have been more sociable.   They took tea with us and did everything they could to make us feel that they desired to help us better our condition.

"This conference was very harmonious.   The masters had to make some concessions and we had to make some.   When this expires in May, 1899, there will probably be a great struggle on account of the situation in Auckland.   The workers there are miserably paid.   We have spent £300 ($1500) in the effort to organise the shirt-makers and tailoresses of Auckland. We have sent some of our best leaders there. We sent some girls who were good organisers privately to work in the Auckland factories to leaven the mass, but it was of no use.   There seems to be a most complete apathy among the workingmen and women there.   There is, too, some trade jealousy, for the Auckland people are afraid they may lose some of their business, as the character of the work done in the

South Island is much superior to theirs. The
Dunedin manufacturers would have a genuine
grievance," this working woman said, "if asked
to pay higher wages than are paid by the Auckland manufacturers, who are their competitors."

We shall see later how these fears that the
poor organisation of the workers of Auckland
might threaten the welfare of the workers elsewhere, were justified. On account of the disorganised condition of the Auckland operatives
and the intractability of some of the Auckland
employers the private peace which had been arranged in the shirt-making and other factory
and clothing industries by voluntary effort
broke down, when the agreement ran out in
May, 1899, as the Secretary of the Dunedin
tailoresses had apprehended.

It was the factory workers who were so successful in Dunedin and Christchurch and Wellington in arranging an agreement until May,
1899.

Whether because their conditions of employment were not so deplorable, or whether for
some other reason they did not receive the same
public support, the girls and women employed
in the tailor shops of Dunedin and Wellington,
though of a higher class industrially, did not
succeed in holding their ground.

While their sisters, the shirt-makers, occupying a lower place in the trade, were enjoying peace, under the terms of their private conciliation, the tailoresses of the shops were compelled to go to the Conciliation Board in April, 1898, in Wellington, and in March, 1899, in Dunedin.

The board, in making its award, took occasion to note that the difficulties it had encountered in the case, which had been very serious, had arisen not at all "from any ill feeling or want of forbearance on either side—because the manner in which the dispute had been conducted was most praiseworthy"—but from technical obstacles peculiar to the trade.

To overcome this, they had made an adjournment for a fortnight and had had an expert from each side to assist them. All these efforts, however, "to get the parties closer to one another" failed.

As the board did not award the Wellington tailoresses the wages they felt they ought to have, their union decided to refuse to accept the award of the Conciliation Board, and the matter went before the Court of Arbitration.

The court, before undertaking to make a decision of its own on the question, adjourned as the Conciliation Board had done, to see if a private arrangement could not be made between the parties. This proved impossible, and, after hearing evidence from both sides, the court made its award.

In this it practically adopted the recommendations of the Conciliation Board. The minimum wage, for instance, for coat-makers was put at £1 10s. ($7.50), the figures fixed by the Conciliation Board; not so much as the working women had asked for, £1 17s. 6d. ($9.37), but more than the masters had been willing to concede £1 5s. ($6.25).

The Arbitration Court also reaffirmed the preference of employment for members of the union, which had been strongly opposed by the master tailors and, to put an end to sweating, stipulated that all work must be done at the shop of the employer.

This award settled the conditions of the trade from September, 1898, to September, 1900. As a result of this arbitration, Miss Whitehorn said, "We are a lot better off than we were."

In Dunedin, as in Wellington, the tailoresses employed in the merchant tailors' shops were compelled to go to the Court of Arbitration, while the shirt-makers were happily at peace as the result of their private negotiations with their employers.

The Dunedin tailoresses were before the Court of Arbitration while I was in Dunedin. Their representative, in his address to the court, gave

an account of the past efforts of employers and
employés to harmonise the trade, and of the new
conditions which had broken down their private
peace.   The agreement which was made after
1892, between the employers and employed had
lasted, he said, for some years, a fact which
showed the good feeling that existed, but things
had now changed.

A large number of new firms had come in,
new methods of business had been introduced,
many of the old abuses prevalent before the in-
ception of the union and its successful negotiation with the masters, such as sweating, low
wages and long hours were beginning to make
themselves felt again.

Both the members of the union and many of
the more important employers had come to the
joint conclusion that, in the interest of both of
them and of the public, a new settlement should
be made, otherwise things would revert to the
unfortunate condition of ten years ago.

In pursuance of this joint understanding, the
representatives of the union and of their employers, the Master Tailors' Association, spent
twelve months in holding meetings and con-
ferring.   As a result of these combined efforts,
they had succeeded in preparing another "log."
Out of forty-nine employers in Dunedin, forty-
two had signed this "log" as satisfactory to
them.   There were only seven who stood out.

An appeal was made to the Conciliation Board. This decided in favour of the agreement made by the union and the forty-two employers, but the other seven remained obdurate, and the Court of Arbitration had to be called upon to make the decisive award.

One of the by-products of arbitration made its first appearance in this case. It indicates an unexpected use of arbitration, and shows the benefits that accrue to the community from compulsory publicity.

Some of the seven employers who would not come into line in the agreement, held out, as the representative of the working women showed the court, because this agreement would put an end to a fraud which was being practised in their shops on the public. They were in the habit of taking orders for clothing to be made according to measure, by first-class workers. But, as a matter of fact, they sent the order to a factory, to be made up by factory workers at factory prices, instead of sending it to their own tailors and tailoresses. They pocketed the difference of this fraud on their customers, or used the money they thus saved in cutting prices, to the detriment of competitors who honestly gave the customer what he paid for.

The court put a summary stop to this sort of deception. In referring to this, the court said in its decision:

"All bespoke work—all goods made and sold as tailor-made; also any order in which there is a garment fitted on—shall be done in the shop of the employer"—and the court ordered that it should be paid for at shop and not factory prices.

The court drily remarked to the representatives of this irreconcilable minority of the employers that, "They would have to come in under the same conditions with the other members of the trade, if they were going to continue in the tailoring business."

This incident shows us the Compulsory Arbitration law working steadily as a force for honesty in trade.   It does so because of the publicity it insures.   The workingmen know and often resent the deceits they are compelled to perpetrate. These are often, as in this case, an injury to them as well as the consumer for they are forced to do inferior work at inferior prices or to see work they should do go to others as in this case.

The open court-room of compulsory arbitration gives them a chance to let out the "trade secret" and protect both the public and themselves.   Where there is an Arbitration Court, manufacturers will think twice before they make coffee with beans, sugar with glucose, or scamp the hidden side of their work, for their working-

men may some day come before the court and let
the public into this awkward secret of "my business."

The decision of the court fixed the lowest
rate of wages to be paid to workers at £1 5s.
($6.25) a week.   It limited the number of ap-
prentices to one to every three operatives.   The
hours were fixed at forty-five in each week.
Overtime was to be paid for at the rate of time
and a quarter, and in case of piece-work, there
was to be 2d. (4 cents) an hour extra.   No ma-
chinist was to machine for more than thirteen
workers, and the employers were required to
employ competent members of the union in preference to non-members.

New difficulties are, of course, continually
arising in the application of the procedure of
compulsory arbitration to business competitors.

One such difficulty arose in the case of the
arbitration between the master tailors of Wellington and their employés.   Two of the firms
protested against being bound by the award, on
the ground that, as it fixed the conditions of
business for two years, new-comers in the trade,
who were not subject to the award, could compete against them on unfair terms, but the court
found a way to meet this just objection.

It directed that these objectors should be
bound by the agreement just as all the others in

the trade were, but stipulated that the union, if any new-comers appeared in the trade, who attempted to under-cut the terms fixed in the decision, should "take the necessary steps to compel them to do so, within fourteen days after notice."

"If the union fails," the decision continued, "to commence and carry out proceedings, or, if in taking such proceedings, it shall be unable to compel such persons or firms to conform with the terms," then all of the employers were to be released.

In this way the court placed upon the union the burden of seeing that all employers, new-comers as well, were brought under the same conditions. The workingmen could easily do this because, under the terms of the Arbitration law, they can proceed against any employer.

Justice was thereby secured to all the employers in the trade, and the initiative, in seeing that this was done and their own interests protected as well, was properly left to the trade-unions, which had been the prime movers in resorting to the Court of Arbitration.

It is time now to turn to Auckland and the part of marplot which it played in the prosperity of the women who sing the Song of the Shirt, as the secretary of the union foretold would happen. The ferment in the public conscience which had done so much for the women workers of Dunedin and Wellington, in 1892, began to work at the same time in Auckland.

The Honourable W. T. Jennings, when the Auckland shirt-makers and other clothing operatives came before the Conciliation Board in November, 1897, made a statement of their efforts for many years and of the assistance which they had received.

The movement in Auckland began a little later than that in Dunedin. How much need there was for it was abundantly shown by facts which were brought to light in 1892. The rate of pay was very low. Cases were discovered of young women who had been years at the trade and were fairly good workers, who received only 9s. ($2.25) a week. The evidence of the operatives showed that the average was about 10s. ($2.50) a week, and the hours for work were a good deal over ten.

A union was formed in 1892, but the manufacturers fought it by discharging the leaders, and, in fact, any of the operatives who could be found to be members.

The knowledge of this intimidation and of the wretchedness out of which sprang this effort of the shirt-makers to organise, led many of the best men and women in the community to come to their help. A public meeting was held under the auspices of the most influential citizens, and the then President of the Auckland Chamber of Commerce, in his address declared it to be the duty of every citizen to recognise the evils of under pay and intimidation, and to rise to the duty of seeing that the weaker section of the community received protection.

Among the other citizens who assisted this movement were a number of employers. Many of them did so, said Mr. Jennings, "believing that it would be conducive to better trade, and would also tend to counteract in a marked degree the 'cutting' practices that prevailed."

There were many conferences between the working girls and their employers, but after protracted delays, the negotiations broke down, and the trade reverted to the anarchy of preceding years.

But after the Compulsory Arbitration law was passed, the working girls renewed their complaints, the union was resuscitated, and negotiations with the manufacturers were resumed.

After ten months hard work, a "log," or schedule of wages was prepared that was acceptable to both employers and the union. There were, however, five employers who refused, like the minority of employers in Dunedin, to concur in the "log," and the Auckland Tailoresses

Union, therefore, as a last resort submitted the matter to the Board of Conciliation.

In stating their case to the Board of Conciliation, their representative spoke as much in the name of the manufacturers who had agreed to the new wages as in that of their employés.

"It is undoubtedly wrong," he said, "that honourable and fair-dealing manufacturers who are prepared to pay a fair wage to their employés should have to compete against others who are working their factories at a difference of over thirty per cent. in the wages of their women workers. There has not been any spirit of antagonism in this matter. It is a battle really in behalf of those who are prepared to do the right thing and to keep down the extension of the sweating system."

The Secretary of the Union, Mrs. Hendre, also addressed the court, and emphasised the fact that, in making this schedule of wages, they had been treated with consideration by many of the manufacturers, and that she therefore hoped this dispute would be amicably decided.

She pointed out that the justice of the claims made by the union was proven by the fact that they had been conceded by a number of the firms.

"We are not asking even now," she said, "what the southern girls are getting."

This co-operation of the better class of employers with the employés was practically universal throughout the clothing trade, and I found it existing in many of the other trades. Speaking on this subject, the Honourable John Rigg said in the Upper House of the New Zealand Parliament:

"The employers see that where the conditions of competition are on an equal basis, the competition is a better one and a healthier one, and fairer.   They suffered more under the old state of affairs where it was possible for a man to sweat his employés, and by this means cut down prices to such a stage that other employers could not follow him.

"I know of instances where the employers are working now hand-in-glove with the unions for the purpose of keeping up organisation and arbitration.   An agreement to that effect was arrived at between the Federated Tailoresses and the Federated Employers, representing Dunedin, Christchurch and Wellington, and the employers are not only assisting the union in many matters, but especially in using their influence to get their employés to go into the unions."

The tailoresses were successful in their appeal to the Conciliation Board, and its award seems to have been accepted, as no further proceedings appear to have been taken.

This award stipulated that the manufacturers must find employment for all competent members of the trade-union before they gave work to those outside the union. The increase in pay allowed the tailoresses in Auckland averaged fifteen per cent.

A great lift was given by these efforts to a trade which had been as depressed in New Zealand as it is through the rest of the world.

But the course of events at Auckland after this award expired was not so favourable. It justified the fears of the secretary of the Dunedin tailoresses as to the effect upon her constituency of the weakness of labour in Auckland. It also clearly exemplified the superiority of a compulsory tribunal over voluntary conciliation in assuring peace. In 1899, the Auckland tailoresses, coming again to a difference with their employers, did not go to the Court of Arbitration as before. After a long private negotiation, they and the employers agreed upon a "log" by themselves.

In the report of this which appeared in the Auckland papers of June 2, 1899, the members of the union were described as jubilant because several important increases had been obtained.

"As it has been accepted," the Auckland News said, "by all parties concerned, there will be no necessity to go to the Board of Conciliation."

But signs soon showed that the workers would have done much better for themselves and for their associates and the rest of the colony, if they had gone to the court instead of attempting to make this private settlement. For in it the shirt-makers and tailoresses of Auckland were clearly outgeneraled by their employers. Before the Board of Conciliation they had secured preference of employment for trade-unionists, but, in this agreement by private conciliation, the manufacturers bound themselves only "not to discriminate against members of the union."

The Auckland employers were evidently shrewdly advised, and, it is probably safe to guess were acting in concert with the associated manufacturers of the rest of New Zealand. By thus getting rid of the preference to trade-unionists and obliging themselves only not to discriminate against unions—a very different thing— they effected a breach in the defences of the crganised clothing workers of the colony.

That this private settlement with the clothing workers of Auckland was but the first of a series of manœuvres to undo, at least in part, what had been accomplished in behalf of all the sewing women of New Zealand before the Board of Conciliation and Arbitration Court, appears from subsequent developments which took place immediately.

The radicals among the employers in New Zealand are against trade-unions, first, last and all the time, as they are in the rest of the world, and they have always made their strongest fight, both outside and inside the Arbitration Court, against the obligation to employ all the trade-unionists before they employed any non-unionists.

Hardly had the Auckland tailoresses made this settlement by private conciliation, in which they foolishly waived the preference for unionists, than the manufacturers everywhere proceeded to take advantage of it.

The New Zealand Clothing Manufacturers' Association, representing the manufacturers of the whole colony, gave notice to the Board of Conciliation that its services were needed in an industrial dispute between themselves and the Federated Tailoresses and other trade-unions in the clothing industry. They significantly submitted with this notice a copy of the new "log" which had been just made by private agreement in Auckland, as a basis upon which they desired a settlement of the dispute.

It is evidently their intention to use the weakened position of the Auckland tailoresses as a standard of comparison by which to bring down the wages and conditions of employment of all the shirt-makers and clothing makers throughout the entire colony. They will undoubtedly use the surrender of the preference for unionists by the Auckland working women as a precedent to induce the court to take away the preference from the workers in the rest of the country.

This is one of the few cases in which associations of manufacturers have initiated arbitration proceedings. So far, in most of the suits, the manufacturers have been on the defensive and the workingmen have been seeking the court, but now, when the manufacturers see a possibility of advantage for themselves, they are quick to appeal to the Arbitration law for its help.

This retreat of the working women of Auckland, from their strongest line of defence—unionism—and the ominousness of the instantaneous appeal of the clothing manufacturers of the entire colony to the Court of Arbitration to make the same terms for all the shirt-makers and other clothing workers as the Auckland manufacturers have made for those in Auckland, have roused the working women of the southern cities to renewed efforts to retrieve the situation.

A circular comes to hand as I write, issued by Miss Whitehorn, the secretary of the Dunedin branch of the tailoresses' trade-unions of New Zealand. In this circular she says the tailoresses of Wellington, Christchurch and

Dunedin are threatened at the present time by their employers with a reduction of their present low rate of wages on account of the keen competition of the Auckland manufacturers. The Dunedin Conciliation Board is reluctant to lower the existing rates of wages, yet it feels that it cannot help doing so unless the Auckland manufacturers and operatives are dealt with in some way to equalise conditions north and south.

Miss Whitehorn repeats what she said to me with regard to the efforts which her union has been making for ten years to place Auckland on the same basis of wages as other parts of the colony, as "they recognise it is only fair to all concerned that equal pay for equal work should be applied to all manufactured clothing in the colony, but unfortunately our efforts have proved unavailing."

Her circular then goes on to show that the Arbitration Act in its present state does not give any help in solving this difficulty. An important amendment to the act is needed and this has therefore been drafted for the tailoresses of the southern cities, and the representative of their district in Parliament has consented to introduce it. It applies of course to all trades.

The amendment provides that as soon as by voluntary or compulsory arbitration certain terms have been established for a majority of the employers in any trade, these same terms may be made binding on all the rest in the trade throughout the colony.

The effect of this amendment, if adopted, will be that, since the majority of the New Zealand clothing trade have already, in Wellington, Dunedin, Christchurch, been brought into agreement with the tailoresses through the Court of Arbitration, the manufacturers of Auckland, though not members of this majority, can be compelled by the court to give their tailoresses the same pay and the same conditions as the other manufacturers.

This addition to the law will give the Court of Arbitration power to enforce on the minority terms acceptable to a majority.   Thus the court can compel a minority of the employers in any business to accept and abide by the same terms for their working people as those agreed upon by a majority of their competitors.   Compulsory arbitration here, again, means government by the majority.   Under this majority rule, the lowering of wages now imminent throughout the entire colony in the clothing trade, by such tactics as those pursued by the minority of Auckland manufacturers would be rendered impossible.

Since the act has been invoked in the clothing trades, nothing like the piteous and unavailing uprising which took place among the women workers in New York a year ago is possible in New Zealand. There have been, as we have seen, continual differences in the trade, but there have been no strikes, and no need for them. None of the disturbances has taken on a more violent character than that which we can observe in the proceedings of any reasonable debating society. Higher wages, uniform terms, better conditions, a cessation of throat-cutting competition have all been the beneficent results. This is at least a humaner manner of warfare, even if we have to admit that it is still warfare.

Even if the plan of campaign of the Auckland manufacturers and their fellow members in the manufacturers' association proves successful and they are able to use the concessions weakly made by the operatives in Auckland, to take from the sewing women of the whole country some of the gains won from the Arbitration Court, it will still remain true that the result of arbitration has been a great uplift in the condition of these distressed workers. The sweater has been sent to the right-about. He may yearn as he will for the return of the "good old times," and for the music so sweet to his ears of the Song of the Shirt as it used to be sung, but he will yearn in vain. In New Zealand the old Song of the Shirt is a "lost chord."

The relations between employer and employed are still those of contest.   It is still a battle that might be to the strong, a race that might be to the swift; but the difference between the two kinds of struggle is the difference between a fair fight in an open field and a massacre.

Under the old procedure of the old Song of the Shirt, the members of the New Zealand Manufacturers' Association, as soon as the Auckland manufacturers had made the breach we have described in the ranks of the Auckland operatives, would have cut down wages throughout the rest of the colony, and would have worsened the hours and the conditions of employment at their own sweet will.

The working women would have had the choice between starving rapidly and starving slowly.   Whether they struck or worked on, they would have to retreat from the room in the second story to one in the attic or the cellar, from a scanty table to one still scantier.   They would have made their last stand where the visitors of the poor find the sewing women singing their song, with a cup of tea and a crust of bread.

But now, around the sewing women of New Zealand all the powers of government and society have drawn the protecting ring of the state.   There are some printed pages, beginning

Be It Enacted, on the shelves of Parliament, there are a few men in a new court-room who now have to be reckoned with by the manufacturer before he can cut those wages and start the women on their way back to the tea and the garret and the crust.

Now he must come out before the public, and in the presence of experts and judges, he must tell why he would do these things. He cannot deceive the public with glowing accounts of the immense wages that his women make. Whatever he ventures to assert on this subject, he must prove, and he must prove it before men accustomed to weigh such statements, and who know all about the lies that figures can be made to tell. And they will look at his books, too, if they think it best to do so in the interests of truth and humanity.

Meanwhile, along with this inquiry in the new court-room, the work goes on. The sewing woman stays where she is in the factory kept clean and light and wholesome by the state, and she does not have to strike; she cannot be locked out; her work cannot be taken from her; her wages cannot be cut down.

This is the new Song of the Shirt,

CHAPTER V.

THIS LAW OF PARLIAMENT BECOMES A LAW OF TRADE.

By this time the observant reader will have made the discovery which I made—a discovery which will do more to explain the compulsory arbitration of New Zealand than all the controversial matter he can find in the newspapers, or in all the political economies. Compulsory arbitration has been a success in New Zealand because the people wanted to arbitrate.

The New Zealand people exhausted private effort to establish arbitration as we have seen in several trades. When they failed repeatedly in these private efforts and discovered that, though a majority wanted arbitration it was continually defeated by an intractable minority, they, as was natural, being also a democratic people, got arbitration for themselves by the political instrument at hand in their democracy—i. e., by a law. Law is the instrument through which democracy equips a majority to maintain its welfare against the attacks of an anti-social minority.

It is, of course, an evil to need to have "laws." But it is a greater evil to have an anti-social minority knocking holes in the bottom of the ship. If the Tolstoians will abolish the scuttling minority, we will abolish the "law based on force."

This pre-disposition of the New Zealand people for arbitration argues a high intelligence and a high character and high political vigour—the intelligence to see the waste and inaccuracy of battle-field arbitration, the character that prefers kinder and juster ways, and the virility to use their votes to execute their will.

We see in New Zealand, in case after case, that the New Zealanders are an arbitrating people. Arbitration was not sprung on them by theorists, or an innovating minority. The business men were moving in that direction, and, if they could have succeeded privately, they would not have had to have a law. The law was a success with them simply because it expressed and effectuated an opinion which the people had already formed. It satisfied a need of which they were already conscious.

A compulsory arbitration law for a people not yet developed enough for the majority to seek to arbitrate voluntarily, would be a folly. Equally, to say that among a people where the majority wanted to arbitrate, a compulsory arbitration law would be unnecessary, is to contradict the obvious fact that an unappeasable minority can, under the voluntary system, defeat arbitration, and can do it, as Mr. Reeves said to the New Zealand Parliament, for generation after generation. The compulsion is not needed for the people in such a case, but for the minority who are defying and outraging the people.

Here the New Zealanders show themselves to be, as in many other things, of the newest Anglo-Saxondom, for the Anglo-Saxon has always been a pioneer in arbitration, though he still fights too much.

The only insuperable difficulties about compulsory arbitration have been the imaginary ones; all the real difficulties have been surmounted one by one as they appeared. The great bugbears of the disbelievers have been, "You cannot make men work by act of Parliament," and "You cannot fix prices by law."

I found the opponents of compulsory arbitration in New Zealand getting great comfort from the arguments against it which were furnished by the London Times in a controversy then on between it and the Agent-General of the colony in London, Mr. Reeves, the author of the law. A number of distinguished men took part in the controversy, the Bishop of Hereford, Lord Monkswell, Lord Thring, and others well known in the English world of thought and action, and an anonymous correspondent, "R," whose communications were always given the place of honour by the Times, and who was well understood to be Lord Rosebery. The articles were widely reprinted in the colony, and discussed everywhere.

The subject came up one day in a group at the club in Wellington. One of the critics of the law quoted triumphantly from a letter of Lord Thring's.

"Is it conceivable that at the close of the nineteenth century either masters or men would submit to such a tyrannical judicial interference with their liberty?"

"For five years," replied one of the New Zealanders, "masters and men have been submitting. They may not be satisfied. Where anywhere are there satisfied capitalists or labourers? Where is there an employer who would not like to pay less, where the workingman who would not like to get more? But they are all at work, though not satisfied. In New Zealand it is proved that the Arbitration Court can make decisions which both sides would rather accept than to quit, as they always have the right to do.

"The London Times, from which you get this remark of Lord Thring's," the speaker continued, "says that, if a court makes an intolerable award, employers will close their doors. In this the Times is quite right. It is therefore the strongest possible commendation of the act in its theory and practice that the employers do not close their doors, but keep on doing business and making money, and this, too, although the awards have almost all been against them.

"We all know that there have been numbers of withdrawals from business in England on account of strikes. As a result of the strike of the Amalgamated Society of Engineers a year ago, some very important concerns that I know of moved their works to Russia and Belgium and other countries. There have been no such withdrawals from New Zealand on account of the 'tyranny' of our Arbitration Court.

"Our position in New Zealand is this: Industry is a joint enterprise. We say to the capitalists:

" 'You and the labourer and the consumer and the public are all interested. We—the state— are the only agency known to society which can protect and harmonise all these interests, provided always that you cannot or will not harmonise yourselves. We cannot leave you to settle with each other in the old way, for that we know by experience leads to strikes, devastation, hate, and even bloodshed. In this world of capitalists, labourers, consumers, and citizens, you, the employing capitalists are a very small minority. We don't propose to sacrifice you or do you any injustice, but, rest assured, neither do we intend to allow you to do us any wrong or injustice. You can stay in this business or go out of it, as you choose. You can go into any business you prefer, but, if you stay in business in New Zealand, you must settle your irreconcilable differences between yourselves and your men by reference to a disinterested arbiter, and not by strikes or lockouts. You can have an arbiter of your own, if you prefer, but an arbiter you must have, and we will furnish the arbiter, if you do not find one for yourselves.'

"Of course," he went on, "some of the capitalists at first, as they always do, said they would 'leave the country,' but our reply was:

" 'Those are the only terms on which you can do business in New Zealand. If you don't like it, leave.'

"But they did not leave. They stay, they arbitrate, and they prosper."

A man prominent in labour matters here took up another point in Lord Thring's letter.

"In the same article Lord Thring asks," he said, " 'Suppose one thousand men refused to obey an award and would not go to work on the terms it prescribed, is it within the range of possibility that the court would be able to imprison and fine one thousand men without producing riots more injurious than the strike?'

"We see the capitalists," the labour man said, "all over the world succeed in forcing the workingmen to go to work on terms unsatisfactory to them.   Are we to suppose that the state is less powerful than the capitalists?   And are not the workingmen more likely to obey a decision in the making of which they have been represented than in one made by the capitalists who would not receive their delegates, nor listen to a word from their side?   The workingmen certainly would riot and smash things, if the decision were absolutely intolerable.   In the last five years in Europe and America there have been riots, arson, and even dynamite in consequence of decisions forced on labour by capital, but nowhere has there been a breath of disturbance in New Zealand on account of any decision forced on labour by arbitration, and labour has had to submit to some things from the Arbitration Court which it found very hard to accept."

In the same conversation the London Spectator was quoted as expressing the opinion that compulsory arbitration made slaves of the workingmen :

"If wages are fixed by the external authority of a court, the individual workman must accept them, that is, must become practically a slave for the benefit of the community."

"The workingman has no choice, in any case with or without arbitration," his representative retorted, "but to 'accept wages that are fixed.' The only practical question for him is, how are they to be fixed?   In the world of strikes and lockouts, he usually has to submit to wages fixed by force, economic violence, which denies him hearing, information, the right to organise, or even recognition.

"In the case of arbitration he submits to a decision given by the nearest approach to a disinterested outsider that human ingenuity can provide.   The decision is based expressly upon the recognition of his equality of rights, and on the fullest examination by him and for him of every book, paper and person necessary for the discovery of all the facts affecting his interest. The workingmen of New Zealand like that kind of 'slavery.'   They are practically all registered, and the employers like the same kind of 'slavery,' for the most important of them are registered under the law—the shoe manufacturers, the clothing manufacturers, the great coal companies, the steamship owners, and many others."

The letters of "R," whom everybody believed

to be Lord Rosebery, came in for their share of
attention. "R," speaking of what would happen, if the court made a decision intolerable
either to workingmen or employer, had said:

"In either case, the award is a dead letter; the
court is impotent, and the law of the market is
supreme, as it was in the beginning and ever
shall be."

A friend of Mr. Reeves who was present read
the reply which Mr. Reeves had made to "R" in
the Times.

"Why assume that the awards of a competent
tribunal will be intolerable to one side or the
other? It is likely enough, nay, certain, that all
awards must be disagreeable to somebody, but
intolerable is a word which pre-supposes that
awards are likely to be made which will involve
one side or the other in ruin, or drive it to des-
peration."

To this he added the remark which Mr.
Reeves made in answer to the same objection
when the bill was before Parliament.

"This court may be assumed to have common
sense and not to be composed of unreasonable
madmen."

"Moreover," Mr. Reeves' friend continued,
"the law of arbitration has now become part of
the 'law of the market.' The New Zealand
theory is that a judge, skilled in the examin-

ation of facts and in the disentanglement of controversies, assisted by experts from both sides, and by additional experts if needed, can tell better what the 'law of the market' is than the employers or employés, drunk with greed, passion or stupidity. Compulsory arbitration does not attempt any interference with the 'law of the market.' On the contrary, it gives the 'law of the market' for the first time a full chance to work. It brings the 'law of the market' into full and free discussion. It offers experts who know the 'law of the market' best on both sides to tell all they know about it. It gives it publicity and debate. It is true the arbiter makes the decision, but a decision must be made anyhow, and has been made heretofore in most cases by the casting vote of suffering, selfishness, or passion. The casting vote of Judge Edwards is better, we New Zealanders think."

There was a senator present, one of the Liberals, and a man who claimed to be a friend of the law, but he insisted that "its compulsion made it odious," and he argued that "public opinion should be the only force behind the law."

One of the most successful business men and large employers in New Zealand said in reply to him:

"The compulsory feature of the law is a necessity, for it fixes the moral position of the parties, if they should either of them break through the award.   Our reliance that awards will not be unreasonable can safely rest upon the general common sense of the court and the public."

And the labour member said as to this point:

"As for the force of public opinion, which you are so anxious to have as the only force behind the award, we will agree to that as soon as public opinion is made the only force behind all other laws, and no sooner."

The labour member was a trifle bitter in private conversation afterwards, in his comments upon this liberal.   He accused him of being one of those who tried at the preceding session of Parliament, under the cover of friendship for the law, to cripple its most important provision, next to compulsory arbitration, that is, preference to trade-unions, by having the title amended so as to strike out the words, "to encourage the formation of industrial unions and associations."

The amendment was made, but the court, as I have explained elsewhere, continued in its policy of giving the trade-unions preference wherever possible.

"You will not find opponents of the law like him," said the labour member, "declaring themselves against its arbitration but only against its compulsion. All the enemies of the law, in fact, avow themselves passionate devotees of arbitration, and all they ask is that the compulsion shall be stricken out of the law, so that they can give the world the magnificent spectacle of voluntary arbitration for which they yearn. But these same men refused arbitration when it was not compulsory. At the worst, the compulsion, we think, can do them no real harm, since it only forces these devotees of arbitration to do what they profess to be willing to do without the law. If they had given us conciliation when it was in their power, we would not have asked for compulsion."

It is plain that the vast majority of the people of New Zealand are not at all shocked by the "compulsion" on which so many changes are rung by the opponents of the law. They regard "compulsion" as a very proper instrument to be used by democracy when it is necessary to protect the rights of the majority against the minority.

"We cannot understand," was said to me, "why compulsion cannot be used to prevent economic crime as well as any other crime, or to repel economic invasion of one class by another, which is just the same thing, for all intents and purposes, as the invasion of one country by another."

The compulsion, too, is defended by citing the precedents given by the factory acts, the laws for the regulation of mining, sanitary conditions and other labour matters, the regulation of railroad rates in all civilised countries. In one of the cases before the Arbitration Court, the judge said:

"There is coercion in everything, and the only question is, where is coercion to begin, and where is it going to end. A man is not allowed to ride his bicycle along the footpath; he is coerced into riding along the muddy road."

In a debate in Parliament on the compulsory feature of the law, one of its defenders quoted the words of William Pitt, when speaking on the Arbitration Act of his day, which was analogous in principle to the New Zealand law.

"The time will come when manufactures will have been so long established, the operatives not having any other position to fill, that it will be in the power of any one man in a town to reduce wages and all the other manufacturers must follow. If ever it does arrive at this pitch, Parliament, if it be not then sitting, ought to be called together, and, if it cannot redress your grievances, its power is at an end. Tell me not that Parliament cannot. Its power is omnipotent to protect."

"It is not a choice," one of the group said,

"between compulsion and no compulsion; it is a choice between two kinds of compulsion, that of a court, or that of labourers or capitalists, resorting to what Mr. Reeves, in urging the bill, called their 'sacred right of insurrection.'"

"After all," urged another, "the compulsion is voluntary. The contestants are free to have their own arbitrator, if they choose, but, if they will not choose one, the people will do it for them. Disinterested men can be found, and disinterested men can find the truth. By giving this duty of disinterested decision to a Judge of the Supreme Court, more honest, competent and just than the average citizen, the state guarantees that the decision by compulsory arbitration will be in the long run more advantageous to the warring parties than one made by themselves.

"The compulsion is not for the majority, but for the minority. The majority both of employers and employés in many trades wanted to arbitrate, but they could not until this law was passed, because the minority would not. As in other laws so in this, compulsion is not for the good men, but for the bad men. Good citizens do not feel that they pay their taxes under compulsion, they are willing to pay, and they are willing to have a compulsory law on the statute book to compel not themselves, but the shirkers."

The gentlemen who were attacking the law, here changed to their other argument.

"You can't fix prices by law, neither prices of labour nor of anything else."

"As a matter of fact," said the labour representative, who had made a similar reply to the similar argument about "the impossibility of making men work by law," "the Arbitration Court does fix prices and fix them so that the employers are willing to pay them, and the employed are glad to receive them. But it is not really correct to say that this is a case of wages 'fixed by law.' The law does not fix the prices. The price is fixed by the facts of the economic situation. By our tribunal, for the first time in any civilised country, the facts of the case can be found, published, and, where there is a dispute, settled by an umpire whose decision all can trust. The law simply sees to it that the decision between conflicting claims as to prices is made by discussion and disinterestedness, and not by force, or fraud, or secrecy."

"Suppose," said an American who was present, "suppose the Court of Arbitration selected by a 'boss' should decide that a dollar and a half for twelve hours' work a day was enough for the men, how would the workingmen like that?"

"How do they like what they get now?" was the answer of the New Zealander, "forced to strike as they are, with no chance of publicity, and to submit to a decision backed by injunctions, Pinkertons, and the military?

"Force to compel a factory to run at a loss would be worth nothing. Force to compel a prosperous manufacturer to reveal his prosperity so that his workingmen may share his prosperity is force that counts for a great deal, and that is where the shoe pinches the men who 'want it all.' The compulsion is not that the manufacturer shall run, but that while he runs, he shall run justly. Society certainly has the right to decree and enforce this. There is no 'fixing wages by law,' no compulsion, no interference, excepting in one contingency. Masters and men are left free to make any agreement they choose; they can negotiate privately; trade-unions can be refused recognition or not; they can mediate their differences by any form of voluntary conciliation or arbitration they like; the employer can give up his business, the workingman can change his occupation. The state says nothing. But the moment one party attempts to force the other, the State of New Zealand can be called in.

" 'Fixing by law' is an odious phrase. How about fixing prices by the fiat of a corporation or a capitalist or by bayonets, or by starvation or intimidation? Here, 'law' means debate; the lack of it means destruction for the men. The

law does not dictate nor fix wages, but merely
decides in a dispute between two different views
of what wages should be. 'Law' fixes creditors'
shares in bankruptcy, lowers Irish and Scotch
rents, fixes the price of ferries, railroads, the
salaries of state officials, rate of taxation.

"Our Arbitration Court simply determines
what is just between two parties under existing
economic conditions. It does not attempt to
create or modify economic conditions. It does
not try to compel either labour or capital to
work, but it does try to prevent either from
throwing upon the other all the burden of the
fluctuations in supply and demand. It will not
allow them to coerce each other by economic
force either of labour or capital. If economic
conditions are such that the industry cannot be
carried on by capital without ruin, or by labour
without starvation, the disputant who is in the
right can easily make the court see that. The
court simply does the best that can be done to
effect a proper distribution of the economic
pressure on the two parties."

The practical ability of the judges and the
consideration they have shown for all sides have
had a great deal to do with making compulsion
workable. The judge, who "knows nothing
of business," sometimes proves to know more
than the business man about his own business.

In one case of which I was told by a distinguished member of Parliament, a labour representative who was the advocate for the men before the court in a dispute between the tailors and their employers, one of the latter declared solemnly that an advance of five per cent. in wages would ruin him.

My informant believes that in making this statement the employer was entirely honest. The decision of the court was in favour of the men, and the advance in wages given was considerably more than five per cent.

Meeting this employer some time afterwards, the labour member asked him how the award had affected him.

"I believe," was his reply, "it will work out all right. We have reorganised our methods and are getting along first-rate."

The judges frequently take occasion to make such remarks as Judge Edwards addressed to the iron moulders. He reminded this union that "the condition of the trade had to be considered, for disaster to the masters would mean disaster to the workers."

And to me, Judge Edwards, in speaking of a decision which he had rendered in the boot makers' case, said that the wages had been fixed by the court as high as they could be, but that they were still altogether too low. But, he said, the court could not fix the wages at a price that would ruin the industry.

In one case the judge refused to shorten the hours on Saturday, "because that would cause inconvenience to other trades."

The Arbitration Law as administered by the judges in New Zealand aims to play within living limits for both employers and employés.

In another case the concession asked for by the employés was refused by the court because, the judge said, it would be "an innovation."

Since the act has gone into operation at a time of expanding industry and rising prices, the applications of the men for higher wages have been uniformly granted, at least in part. But the court has shown itself quite able to discriminate when discrimination was called for.

The Consolidated Gold Fields Company lowered the wages of its men from 10s. ($2.50) to 8s. 4d. ($2.08) a day. The miners held a meeting, discontinued work for three weeks, and then formed themselves into a union and referred their case to the Conciliation Board. Pending its decision, they resumed their work at 9s. ($2.25) a day.

The case went on up to the Court of Arbitration. The judge decided that the reduction of wages had been premature, but, looking to the large amount of money that was being spent by the company in prospecting and opening up new ground, these being non-paying operations, he ruled that the miners should consent to take a lower wage for a limited period, after which they should be permitted to open the whole question. Their wages were therefore fixed at 9s. 6d. ($2.37) a day temporarily.

It has been the aim of the court wherever possible in its awards to make conditions uniform for all parts of the colony for all the members of the trade before it. The court did this in the painting trade. In deciding a much more difficult case, that of the iron moulders of Wellington, the court said:

"It is not difficult to make conditions uniform in such a trade as that of the painters, for they are not in competition with those of distant towns. Increasing the wages of painters and making them the same throughout the colony, does not mean giving an advantage to a painter in Auckland over one in Invercargill. In towns where the wages were raised to the level ruling elsewhere, it means only that the person for whom the business was done had to pay a little more for it."

But the firms in the moulding business, in the various towns of the colony, are in sharp competition with each other. In fixing wages to be paid the employés of the iron moulding firms of

Wellington, the judge said the court ought to be very careful not to cause an interference with trade, and drive it from one part of the colony to the other, a possibility disastrous to employers and employés alike.

The decision fixed the wages of the Wellington iron moulders at 9s. ($2.25) a day, although the same class of employés were paid 10s. ($2.50) a day in Dunedin, and living and rent were cheaper there than in Wellington.

It was no doubt a great misfortune, the court said, that they could not take into consideration all parts of the colony and fix a wage for all— not necessarily the same wage, but one that would do justice to the workers, while not inflicting injustice on employers; but all they could do in this case at present was to see that, while the men got a fair living wage, the masters were not injured.

The court would have liked to see the Wellington iron moulders paid the same wages as those in Dunedin, the judge said, but it was plain they ought not to interfere with the present conditions as to the rate of wages which seemed to be fair wages in Wellington for men of that class. They made the award operative for a year only, as they had done in the competing town of Christchurch a few weeks back. This was in the hope that during the year they would be able to consider the conditions of the trade and their effect upon workingmen in each branch of the trade throughout the colony, and perhaps make an arrangement on a basis which would give satisfaction all around.

When I asked the workingmen of South Australia why practically none of their unions had registered under the Arbitration Law of that colony, the reply was that they were afraid of some of their judges. The large number of New Zealand unions and business men's associations that have organised to qualify themselves to appear before the Arbitration Court shows that they have no fear of that kind.

One of the benefits anticipated from the act was that the very fact that such a law was on the statute books would render appeals to it unnecessary. This has proved so. When both employers and employés know that either can summon the other before a tribunal which has the power to make a decision between them, and to enforce it, they are likely to think twice before they insist on unreasonable demands. They will be careful about running the risk of being involved in proceedings which will cause an expensive waste of time and money.

This news paragraph gives a significant hint of how much surer is the footing of the men when they ask for better terms with an Arbitration Law in the background than elsewhere:

"At a meeting of the employés of the iron

trade in Auckland, a number of masters were also present.   The workers demand shorter hours, better wages, and the regulation of apprentices.   All the employers are to be invited to consider the demands before application is made to the Conciliation Board."

Items like the following are not infrequent in the New Zealand newspapers.

"The furniture workers and employers have come to an agreement to extend the present award for two years."

This was the second time that such a settlement had been made in this trade, and similar occurrences are continually taking place.   These people having once been before the court were so well satisfied with the justice and reasonableness of its decisions, that they renewed it voluntarily without invoking its aid.

I was in Dunedin when an even pleasanter incident brought into view one of the unexpected uses of the new tribunal.

The printing trade there as everywhere was being revolutionised by a typesetting machine, and the typographical union had sued their employers, the two principal dailies, in the new court.   The men's case had to be thrown out for a fatal defect in their procedure, but, having come together, neither side liked the idea of separating with nothing accomplished.

"Although the court could do nothing officially, perhaps it would have no objection to see if it could do something unofficially?"

No sooner said than done. The judge was willing and an informal conference was held in which all joined. This friendly talk led to a further meeting in the evening of a more deliberate character. This was attended by the judge, the other members of the court, representatives of the typographical associations, and the employers. Judge Edwards presided, and the Otago Daily Times of Dunedin says in its report, "gave some impartial and friendly counsel to the parties to the dispute, urging them to settle their differences, if it were at all possible for them to do so. Employers and men expressed their appreciation of the disinterested service rendered, in an unofficial way by the president of the court, and the result, after a protracted discussion, was the arranging of a further meeting to be held to-day, which, there is some reason to believe, will insure a settlement of the dispute."

The adjourned meeting was held in the morning, and the representatives of the newspapers and the printers met, with full powers to come to an agreement, if they could. After a short discussion, an agreement was arrived at on the same terms as had been agreed to in Christchurch and Wellington, and, says the newspaper:

"It is felt that this amicable settlement is largely due to the kindly intervention of the judge."

The employers conceded one of the principal points of difference, that about men newly put at work on machines—probationers.   It was agreed that they should be paid full weekly wages from the time of starting, £3 6s. ($16.50) for night work, and £3 ($15.00) for day work of seven hours.

A sufficiently dramatic contrast to this picture of amicable and uncostly compromise can be found in the strike which occurred a year or two ago in Chicago, in which all the daily newspapers in the city suspended publication for several days.

Nowhere is the conservatism of the people and of the judges who have the Compulsory Arbitration law to administer better shown than in dealing with that part of the law which relates to penalties.   This has been the last chapter in the development of the administration of the law, and the demonstration of the ability and determination of the judges to enforce penalties when necessary, has given the crowning touch to the stability and dignity of the court.

The penalties for violation of an award were

obviously intended by the law as first passed to be fine or imprisonment, or both, but, through some defect in the drafting, the only penalty which could be enforced was imprisonment. Undoubtedly the fear of so harsh a punishment had its influence in keeping those subject to the award in line, but the workingmen and their friends feared that some case of obduracy might one day occur which would have to be punished, and that if anything so severe as committal to jail were inflicted for the breach of a law so novel, there might be a revulsion of public opinion, and possibly all that had been achieved might be overthrown.

By common consent the law was so amended that fines as originally contemplated could be levied and enforced.   That done, the judges show a firm hand in dealing with offenders.

In deciding the case of the shoe manufacturers outside the manufacturers' association which has been described in a preceding chapter, the court fined them the sum of £5 ($25) each, to be paid to the union of their men as reimbursement of the expense to which they had been put in bringing the employers before the court.

In another case, two mining companies, which had paid their men only 8s. 6d. ($2.12) a day, instead of 10s. ($2.50) a day, which had been awarded by the court, were fined £25

($125.00) each and ordered to pay the wages originally fixed by the court.

A master plumber was brought before the Arbitration Court and shown to have been guilty of three breaches of an award given in the case between him and his employés. He had not paid the wages stipulated, he had employed more than the prescribed number of assistants, and he had neglected to supply his workingmen with tools.

The court took a serious view of the case. It said that it had come to the conclusion that this employer had set out deliberately to disregard its award; he had continued to do so, even after his men had remonstrated with him; his payment of less wages than prescribed was wilful; he had thus been able to enter into unfair competition with other firms. Unless the awards of the court were to become a nullity, it said, a substantial fine must be inflicted. When it could be proved that the persons evading an award reaped pecuniary advantage thereby, the penalty must, as nearly as possible, be figured to deprive them of that benefit.

The penalty would therefore in this case, the first offence, be fixed at £20 ($100). The second breach was found to be only a slight one, and a penalty of 5s. ($1.25) was imposed for that. As to the supply of tools, the court found that the journeymen obtained their tools only with very great difficulty. They were furnished obviously in such a way as to drive them to buying tools out of their pockets in order to retain their employment. But the court, in view of the fines already enforced, would take a merciful view of this breach, it said, and impose a penalty of only £1 ($5).

But the guilty man was also amerced in the payment of £7 7s. ($36.75) costs, which he had to reimburse to the union, and he had in addition to this to pay the witnesses' expenses and the court fees. He was ordered to reimburse the union its costs, the court said, because the hearing of the case had occupied a whole day, and the defence had been wholly without merit. Both employers and workmen must understand, it warned them, that when they occupied the time of the judge and arbitrators in hearing a frivolous defence or a frivolous claim, they would have to bear not only the penalty, but the costs.

A baker, who began work earlier than the hour set by the court to govern the whole trade, was adjudged to have been guilty "of a deliberate infringement," and called upon to pay what the judge described as a "moderate penalty," £10 ($50), besides all the costs.

But when another baker was before the court,

he was dealt with very much more mercifully. He was shown to have been guilty of a persistent breach of the award, in beginning work earlier than his competitors. But the bench would not inflict a very heavy fine, it said, partly "because he did not appear to be in a very large way of business." His fine was therefore made 40s. ($10), but he was also compelled to pay all the costs and court fees.

Some of the workingmen in their applications for the infliction of penalty showed some indications of a vindictive spirit and a desire to get a snap judgment on their employers, but the court was peremptory in rebuking and defeating these attempts.

In one of the disputes in the baking trade, the court found that the employer had been undoubtedly guilty of a breach, but it found also that the union had not begun proceedings against him until some months after the occurrence, and had given him no notice whatever of the alleged breach of the award, and had made no request of him for any explanation. The court thought the course taken by the union suggested rather an undue anxiety to get a case against him than any dread of oppression on his part. It declared itself satisfied that, if the employer had been notified that the wage fixed by the award must be paid, or, if the union had requested the payment of the amount, there would have been no necessity for the present proceedings. However, as there had been a breach of the award, it felt itself bound to impose a penalty, for it was the duty of employers to obey the provisions of the award, without any request by their workingmen.

"Under these circumstances, a fine of 20s. ($5) and court costs will be sufficient to call the attention of employers to the necessity of a strict observance on their part of the provisions of the award, even though no mention of such provisions was made by the workingman, and even though the workingman may be a consenting party to the breach."

The court lectured the representatives of the union severely on their conduct of these cases, and told them that where they had reason to believe that any employer was not acting up to the terms of an award, it was their duty before taking steps to make him a party to quasi-criminal proceedings, to endeavour to come to some amicable settlement with him. If the unions did not do this, they were not acting, the court told them, in the best interests of unionism.

Several similar cases to the one just described have been brought before the court, and it has always made the same ruling. Wherever it finds that the union has proceeded against an employer without making any endeavour to come to an amicable understanding with him, and without giving him any notice to discontinue his objectionable practice, and with no warning that he was to be taken before the court, it has imposed almost nominal penalties.

The employers met the Arbitration Act at first with a great deal of resistance, active and passive. They refused to register under the act, but they found that this did not prevent them from being called into court. They refused to exercise their right of electing representatives for the Conciliation Boards and Courts of Arbitration. The government thereupon exercised its right to make elections for them. They refused to appear before the court. Their cases then went by default.

One of the members of Parliament, who was also a member of one of the Conciliation Boards, told me of a case in which a large corporation, when summoned before the court, began proceedings by dictating as to the methods of procedure to be followed. When they found that they could not have their own way, they declared that they would withdraw. They were thereupon told that they could do so, if they chose, but that if they did, they would be in the same position as any other party before a court— judgment would go against them by default on all points.   They then decided to remain and fight it out.   They did so, and lost.

In this case, notice was given to the company that they must produce either their books or a sworn statement of certain particulars as to their business, which were needed to decide between them and their men.   This ended the proceedings.   To save themselves the production of their books, they at once came to an agreement with their men.   They have since renewed this agreement without the intervention of the court.

One of the important gold-mining companies in New Zealand sought to escape the Court of Arbitration when summoned by its men by pleading that it was not subject to the jurisdiction of the court.

"Our company is registered in Britain and is not resident in New Zealand," the manager said.

But the chairman put this argument aside. "Any one who is an employer in New Zealand can be made a party to these proceedings."

Some of the employers complained to me that they were compelled to go into court on trivial grounds, and that their time and that of the court and the public money was thus wasted, and the author of the law, in his book on New Zealand, "The Long White Cloud," warns the trade-unions that they have shown a tendency to make too frequent a use of it.

The court has the power to dismiss trivial or frivolous cases and to put the costs on the offender. Representatives of the masters are members both of the Boards of Conciliation and the Court of Arbitration, and the masters themselves appear before them and can point out any instances of such litigation.

"We must deal with human nature as it is," one of the labour members said to me in discussing this objection. "Which is better, to leave the fools and mischief-makers to bring on strikes, or to bring on arbitration? Agitators foment disturbances to bring the masters before the court. It is suspected sometimes that even members of the Conciliation Board, who are paid for the number of days they sit, do the same thing. But which is worse, that agitators should foment arbitration, or foment strikes?"

Another objection often made is, that in consequence of the law, industry is disturbed by the frequency of disputes; but when I looked into the number of cases before the court, I found that there had only been about fifty in five years, about one case a month.

This, too, it is only fair to remember, is the number of disputes at the beginning of the administration of the law. Every decision that settles questions makes precedents that will prevent other disputes from being brought forward.

This point about the disturbance of industry was well met by Mr. Reeves in one of his letters to the London Times, in the controversy already mentioned. An Auckland paper had been quoted as authority for the complaint that the act kept the colony in a state of seething industrial ferment. Auckland, as Mr. Reeves pointed out in his reply, is a large and flourishing district, comprising about a fifth of New Zealand:

"But how many disputes were there in the Auckland district during the four years after the passing of the act, that is, from October, 1894, to October, 1898? Two! Two cases in four years!"

When the amending act of 1898 was before the Labour Bills' Committee of Parliament, the only appearance against the bill was made by a business man who was an active leader in organising associations of employers for the purpose of protecting their interests in labour legislation and similar matters. He is the president of one of these associations called the Industrial Corporation of New Zealand.

I got from him an interesting account of the methods pursued by his association in the Maritime Strike of 1890. When the men, seeing that they were beaten, appealed to the government to intercede with the employers to meet them, the government communicated with this association, the Industrial Corporation. Its President, my informant, wired to all the other employers' associations in the country the answer they should make. This was in substance uniform, to wit: That they were satisfied with things as they were. The wording was varied so as not to make it seem that they were all acting in concert, but the substance was the same. The men were defeated.

As a representative of this Industrial Corporation this gentleman appeared before the Labour Bills' Committee, and his statement is printed in its report among the parliamentary papers. His main points were: That the law was unjust to the masters, because, while they had property and could pay any penalty imposed, fines could not be enforced against the trade-unions since they had nothing. That the workingmen could have the law enforced against the employer, but he, in his turn, had no remedy against the employés, if they chose to disobey the award. That you cannot compel men, labourers or capitalists, to work by act of Parliament. That the employers of New Zealand had to compete with employers in other countries, with Argentina, for example, in the export of meat to England, where there were no arbitration laws to hamper their rivals. That the experience of England proved that conciliation, not arbitration, was to be the potent factor in settling trade disputes in the future. Finally, that New Zealand prosperity was declining; the poor were poorer; there were £5,000,000 sterling ($25,-000,000) lying idle in the banks; capital refused to embark in new enterprises. "In my opinion," he concluded, "the unwise measures passed by the New Zealand Parliament are entirely responsible for this." "These infernal bills," he called the Arbitration Acts.

The labour men whom I questioned as to whether it was true that the awards could not be enforced against workingmen made replies that seemed conclusive. A very large proportion of the trade-unionists in New Zealand own their own homes, a larger proportion, perhaps, than in any other country. A penalty of £10 ($50) could certainly be collected from such men. As to the argument that the provision for penalties was useless because no employer would be so cruel as to attempt to have $50 fines levied on recalcitrant workmen, the men laughed at this assumption of soft-heartedness and pointed to the conduct of the employers in New South Wales in sending the leaders of strikes there to jail for years. Trade-unions have the power of collecting dues from their members, which would easily realise the maximum penalty of £500 ($2,500), that can be levied. The boot makers spent £6,000 ($30-000) on one strike before the days of arbitration.

Besides, as one of the members of Parliament said, the workingman who sets out to disobey an award, will not only have to leave town, he will have to leave the district, for the award covers the whole of a district. He will often have to leave the colony, for many of the awards are made to apply to the country at large.

The same point applies to the manufacturer. The court, in making its decision, considers not only the conditions of the individual manufacturer, but those of the whole trade in the district, and, whenever possible, those of the whole colony.

To the suggestion that men in collusion with the trade-union officials might quit work, but receive sick pay, or strike pay, the answer was made that many of the trade-unions had no sick funds, and as for strike pay they could not get that. Every cent of expenditure by a trade-union has to be reported to the registrar of the friendly societies. No expenditure is legal that is not allowed by the rules of the society as registered. For any illegal expenditures, every officer of the union is personally liable.

One change which the Industrial Corporation

sought to have made in the law it obtained.
This was that the words in the title "to encourage the formation of industrial unions and associations" should be stricken out. They wanted
these eliminated to remove one ground on which
the judges had given preference to trade-unions.
They succeeded in getting the change made, but
it has not produced any effect upon the decisions
by the judges. The latest news in January,
1900, is that this association and other organisations of employers are to take this sore point to
the Supreme Court to obtain a decision forbidding the Arbitration Court to continue its preference to trade-unionists. The friends of
arbitration hope this appeal to the Supreme
Court to interfere, will be ineffectual in view of
the explicit language of the act already referred
to, making the Arbitration Court independent of
the other courts: "No award or proceeding of
the Court shall be liable to be challenged, appealed against, reviewed, quashed, or called in
question by any Court of Judicature on any account whatsoever."

CHAPTER VI.

WHAT IT COSTS AND WHAT IT PAYS.

THE total cost of the administration of the Arbitration and Conciliation Act during 1898-9 was £1,359 ($6,795). Of this the Arbitration Court was responsible for £656 ($3,280), the Conciliation Board £734 ($3,670), and the legal expenses were £12 ($60). The total cost to November 1, 1899—four years—has been £4,400 ($22,000).

What did the country get for this expenditure?

The only country in the world where for four years there have been no strikes or lockouts, is the only country where there is a compulsory arbitration law, New Zealand, and New Zealand is to-day more prosperous than it ever has been before, and is, as far as my observation goes, the most prosperous country in the world.

The Otago Daily Times, the leading opposition paper in the colony, said last year:

"It cannot be even plausibly urged that the effect of the Conciliation and Arbitration Act has so far been injurious or damaging."

The Wellington Times says:

"The result has been a great spread of industrial peace."

In the report recently submitted to the Victorian government by the Honourable R. W. Best, its Minister for Lands, of a tour of investigation made by him in New Zealand to study its land and labour laws, he quotes the following to show how some of the principal employers regard the act:

"Speaking at a special meeting of the Dunedin Chamber of Commerce, on October 19, 1897, to consider certain bills then before Parliament, Mr. James Mills, Managing Director of the Union Steamship Company, and one of the largest employers of labour in New Zealand, is reported by the Otago Daily Times to have said that 'personally he thought the Conciliation and Arbitration Act was a very beneficial one and one of the most important that had been passed, and he felt that they were under a debt of gratitude to the present government and Mr. Reeves for maturing the bill in its present shape. Probably the measure was capable of improvement, and it would be improved from time to time, but he was sure that compulsory arbitration was the true solution of all labour difficulties.' "

In an address by the Right Honourable Richard J. Seddon, the Premier of New Zealand, at a representative gathering of London capitalists interested in the mining industry, one of the strongest points which the Premier made to encourage the investment of English capital in New Zealand mines, was the stability given to business enterprise by the Arbitration Law.

"With us," he said, "a strike of the miners is impossible, as it is also impossible for the owner of the mine to shut down.   That is a condition of things which does not prevail anywhere else. There is a safeguard for you.   The result has been this, that even the employers, who were the first to object to that legislation, are to-day the strongest in favour of it, because where they have strikes of any kind where there is a large amount of capital invested, the effect of that capital being laid up for weeks, and exactions being demanded which that capital could not bear, would be as disastrous as it would be to our mining.   The law, as it stands now, has prevented disputes, which, if there had been an industrial struggle, must have meant a loss of about a million of money to us as a small community, whereas, the whole cost of the proceedings, and the whole thing summed up, would not amount to £1,000."

There is a growing tendency in the later cases towards the admission of lawyers, and to a narrower interpretation of its powers by the court itself.

Besides the grocers, the court has in 1900 excluded street-car men and livery stable employés as not engaged in "industrial" pursuits.

The drift of the reasoning of the court appears to be that no occupations are "industrial" except manufacturing.

The workingmen have appealed to government to introduce legislation as soon as Parliament opens to safe-guard the act from such hostile interpretation.

This reasoning of the court would also exclude seamen; and yet the act was expressly passed to make a recurrence of the disastrous Maritime Strike of 1890 impossible.

Common-sense, the New Zealand critics of these decisions say, would seem to insist that where strikes are, there is the field of the law.

The stability which arbitration gives to business contracts in New Zealand is unknown, as its Premier said, to any other business men in the world.   After an award, the New Zealand business man can make his contracts for one or two years ahead, with no fear of any "labour troubles."

The law is, as one of the labour members in the Upper House admitted, a two-edged sword.

It has been cutting in favour of the workingmen in the present rising market; it will cut in favour of the employers in the falling market which must come.

One of the most successful employers and capitalists in the country described to me the situation of the employer under compulsory arbitration as one of "perfect comfort."

"Under the old system," he said, "our differences with our men had to be settled by a brutal fight. Now two committees meet before the court, and meanwhile the industry goes on just as if nothing were the matter."

He quoted to me the manager of one of the largest coal companies in the colony as declaring to him that, although he had always been opposed to the present ministry, he had to admit that this law was a magnificent thing for any statesman to have done for his country.

"We know now just what to count on," he said.

This testimony added to that just given from one of the largest steamship companies, and the attitude of the majority of the manufacturers in the shoe trade, furniture trade, and the clothing trade—among the most important industries of New Zealand—show how favourable the most influential manufacturers of New Zealand are to compulsory arbitration.

I heard of no case in which an employer had been crippled, or an industry hurt, by an award. That there have been no "intolerable" decisions may be fairly inferred from the fact that all the awards have been obeyed, and that in only a very few cases have penalties had to be laid, and these have always sufficed to end the trouble.

When the Arbitration law was before Parliament, one of the leaders of the opposition predicted that "it would cause disturbances in our industrial world which it would be powerless to control."

As a matter of fact, the number of disturbances which have occurred have been limited to a little less than one a month, and the "disturbances" have only been debates before the court. Five years of complete peace is worth something.

The London Times and its correspondent, "R," united in the declaration "that a compulsory arbitration court has no more power to prevent industrial war than an arbitrator mutually chosen under the English system."

Under the New Zealand system industrial war has ceased. Under the English system it continues unabated.

The opinion of the working people is pronounced in favour of the law. Nearly every trade-union in the colony has registered, and many trades that were unorganised have formed themselves into unions to secure its benefits.

At a recent conference of representatives of the trade and labour bodies of the colony held in Christchurch, April, 1899, every proposal for an amendment of the Arbitration Act was voted down, except one in favour of having the employés of the government admitted to its benefits.

More conclusive even than the opinions of leading business men and trade-union conventions, and the principal journals of the colony, and more representative of the opinion of the community as a whole, is the attitude which Parliament has come to take with regard to the Compulsory Arbitration law. It has already been told how the fierce opposition with which the first project of the law was met in 1892, had most of it disappeared as the result of three years' consideration when the bill came to be passed in 1894, and how the bill received the support of the leaders of the opposition.

The operation of the law has brought it into increasing favour. The act was amended in 1896, and again in 1898, and the records of Parliament show that in both cases the amending acts went through without material opposition, or hostile debate.

The amending act of 1898 was an especially

important one, and one which should have
aroused whatever latent opposition there may
have been, for its purpose was to effectuate the
"compulsion" by making the provisions for
penalties in case of disobedience enforceable.
By this time, 1898, the act had been in active
operation for over two years. If there had been
any deep feeling against the law, if real harm
was being done to business, if any poignant
pain was being caused to the lovers of "liberty"
and "freedom of contract," it should certainly
have found expression at that opportunity. But
there was none. Mr. Reeves described what
happened in one of his letters to the London
Times, in December, 1898:

"Only last month a friendly amending act,
meant to clear up and emphasise certain sections
of the act, and cure a legal flaw supposed to have
been found in it, was passed through the House
of Representatives absolutely without any kind
of opposition; yet the session was, perhaps, the
stormiest and most contentious held in the
colony in recent years. This act, somewhat
modified, passed the Upper House. No other
government labour bill did."

The prosperity of the country is incontestable.
Every year, since 1894, manufactures and all
industries have been increasing. The statistics
of deposits in the banks, of the receipts through

the custom-houses, of the accumulation of wealth, the business of the railroads, the settlement of land and the growth of population, the transactions of the post-office, have all revealed a steady improvement. Capital has not fled the country, but is glad to remain among the wingless birds for which New Zealand is famous. Nearly every New Zealand newspaper reports some new enterprise undertaken by capital, domestic or foreign. Friends of the law did not claim to me that it had caused this prosperity, but they pointed out that it completely disproved the predictions that ruin would follow it.

"Arbitration without compulsion is a sham," was the conclusion which Mr. Reeves drew from the studies which he had made of the experiments of other countries, in presenting his bill to Parliament.

The same conclusion is reached in an interesting tract on "State Arbitration and the Living Wage," issued by the Fabian Society of England, which I found being widely read in New Zealand.

"Voluntary arbitration," it says, "can be summed up as a universal failure."

A very remarkable illustration of this is furnished by the condition of things in Denmark at this writing. To break up the building trades' organisations, the masters and builders locked out forty thousand men, one half of the working population of Denmark—as many for Denmark as five millions would have been in Great Britain. The majority of the press, many of the clergymen and leading citizens have sided with the men. Public opinion was overwhelmingly on their side.

There is in Denmark an industrial arbitration court. It was established at the suggestion of the employers, with the consent of the trade-unions. Its judgment was invoked in this crisis, and its decision was for the men and against the masters. But it has no power to enforce its award, and the masters have treated its decision with complete contempt.

The paper of the Fabian Society gives the latest information as to the results obtained by various forms of private arbitration and government voluntary arbitration in different countries.

Boards, like the Durham Joint Committee in England, for the coal trade, have been successful in settling a number of cases, but such instrumentalities exist only in a few well organised trades, and even there they do not settle the worst disputes.

There had been in Great Britain up to the end of June, 1897, nine hundred strikes, which the government conciliation act had failed to prevent or terminate.

In Germany there were four hundred and

eighty-three strikes in the year 1896, which the Industrial Court had no power to prevent. It decided twenty cases, and its award was rejected in eleven others.

The Conseils des Prud'hommes in France has no power to deal with strikes, nor with disputes involving more than $100. Under the law of 1892, in France, which gives powers of conciliation to the Juge de Paix, there were, in the following four years, one thousand nine hundred and six disputes, of which only 9.28 per cent., less than one in ten, were settled successfully. The employers refused mediation in one hundred and sixty nine cases.

The Massachusetts State Board of Arbitration, in 1896, settled sixteen out of twenty-nine cases. The New York State Board was able, in 1896, to settle two per cent. of the two hundred and forty-six disputes which occurred in that state.

At this writing a new strike bill is pending in the German Parliament. To contemplate its provisions is like passing from the mountain air of New Zealand into the torture chamber of some mediæval castle on the Rhine.

The bill provides that any one who attempts by physical force, threats, defamation, or boycott to induce employers or employed to join or not to join unions, or become parties to agreements, the object of which is to influence the conditions of labour or wages, shall be liable to imprisonment not exceeding one year, or, in case of extenuating circumstances, to a fine not exceeding £50 ($250).

Should a strike or lockout be forcibly brought on, or life, or property, or the security of the state jeopardised, the penalty shall be three years hard labour, except in the case of ring leaders, for whom the maximum penalty shall be five years.

No wonder the bill was at once nicknamed the Penitentiary Bill.

Perhaps on the whole the most notable expression of New Zealand public opinion with regard to its Compulsory Arbitration law was made by Judge Williams of that colony, in a letter which he wrote—he was then in London—to the London Times, as a contribution to the controversy then going on in its columns. Judge Williams had been presiding judge of the Court of Arbitration. He was not an elective judge, nor a re-elective judge, which is still worse, and had no occasion to bid for votes even had he been capable of doing so. He was no longer at the head of the Arbitration Court. He belongs, politically and socially, to the class which would be by inheritance and acquirement least likely to be sympathetic with any form of

labour legislation.   There could be no more disinterested, no more intelligent testimony than
his. His letter was widely reprinted by the press
of the colony, and long as it is, it is reproduced
here as a valuable contribution to the literature
of this important question.

"May I add a word to the discussion which is
taking place in your columns on the New Zealand Industrial Arbitration Act?

"I was President of the Industrial Arbitration
Court from the time the act was brought into
operation until April last, 1898, and have had
some experience of its working. With the introduction or the framing of the act I had nothing to do. The act is, of course, imperfect. Any
act dealing with an entirely new and difficult
subject must necessarily be imperfect.   The
statutory law of bankruptcy. as it now exists,
did not spring heaven-born from a single brain,
but has attained its present state of perfection,
or imperfection, only after years of experience
and infinite emendation. I have no doubt also
that mistakes have been made in the administration of the act.   Those who are set to perform a
novel and delicate experiment, however careful
they may be, not infrequently burn their own
and other people's fingers.

"That compulsory arbitration in New Zealand is still in the experimental stage must be conceded; but there are, I venture to think, good grounds for hoping that the experiment will be ultimately successful. It is certainly not time to say that the experiment is a failure.

"When we find that a number of cases have been dealt with under the act, and that since the act has been in operation strikes and lockouts have practically ceased, it is difficult to say that there is no promise of good. That those who know where the shoe pinches are content to wear it is shown by the fact that no political party suggests the repeal of the act, but that both parties in the last session of Parliament gave their best efforts to amending it.

"Opinions, of course, differ; but it will be found that the vast majority of the newspapers in the colony are favourable to the act, and that Parliament, in retaining the act on the statute book, and striving to make it more efficient, faithfully represented the trend of public opinion.

"One good thing the act does is to prevent bitter feeling arising. The moment there is a difference, the intervention of the Conciliation Board is invoked, and, instead of quarrelling among themselves and making a settlement every day more difficult, each lays his case before a third party.

"Unless you interfere the moment a difference arises, you must wait till both parties are sick of fighting.   The futility of interference in the middle of a quarrel is explained by Rabelais in one of his cleanest and most amusing chapters.   In nearly every case that came before the court I was struck with the good temper displayed by all parties.

"Another benefit of the act is that the hearing of the case before the Conciliation Board and before the court enables the public to form an intelligent opinion upon the merits.   If public opinion supported the judgment of the court, it would be difficult for either side, apart altogether from the question of compulsion, to act in defiance of public opinion.

"No doubt the difficulty of the act lies in the clauses which impose a penalty for a breach of the award.   It has been justly said that you cannot compel a workman to work or an employer to carry on his business under conditions which are intolerable to either.   But the duty of the Arbitration Court is to pronounce such an award as will enable the particular trade to be carried on, and not to impose such conditions as would make it better for the employer to close his works or for the workmen to cease working than to conform to them.   The object of the act is to secure industrial peace, and not to create industrial strife.

"I suppose that at present every employer in the Kingdom is working under some conditions with respect to his workmen that he would like to get rid of, and that every trade-union would in the same way like to improve the conditions under which its members are employed.   Yet as both employer and workman get their living by carrying on the business, each prefers to submit to some restrictions rather than risk his livelihood by a lockout or a strike.

"It is, of course, natural for each side to try and get rid of the conditions which in England arise from the relations of the parties, and in New Zealand are imposed by the court.

"The object of the penalty clause is, I take it, to prevent either party from wriggling out of these latter conditions.   It surely cannot be beyond the reach of human ingenuity to make such clauses efficient.   However, on this, as on many other points, we shall be helped by a wider experience.

"As I have said, the act is an experiment, but an experiment with good hopes of success.   In four or five years we shall be able to speak with more certainty.   Even, however, if in New Zealand the act should be permanently successful, it by no means follows that it should succeed under the very different conditions which obtain here.

"The act at any rate is a bold and honest attempt to grapple with one of the most difficult of our social problems, and I submit that its operation is worthy of careful study.   It is yet too early to pronounce a final judgment on our attempt; but even if the attempt should fail, the failure may give light to a better way."

One of the unexpected effects of the new institution is that the benefit of the better wages and conditions established by the Arbitration Court reach other workingmen, though they were not concerned in the proceedings before it.

I learned of a case in which a large contractor had hired a carpenter without specific agreement as to his wages.   When pay day came the workman refused to accept the pay tendered him, as it was less than had been fixed for the trade by recent arbitration.   He summoned his employer before a magistrate not of the Arbitration Court.   This employer, though one of the largest in Wellington, was not a member of the employers' association, and had not been brought under the award which had been made governing the trade; but the magistrate held that that award fixed "the custom of the trade," and that the employer must pay this customary rate of wage.

The judges of the Arbitration Court have done very little legislating under cover of inter-

pretation, as courts have been known sometimes
to do, but in their decisions there is a clear tendency towards the establishment of some new
principles in business. It would be inevitable
that something of the kind should be developed
when an institution so novel and so powerful
was introduced into the belligerent chaos of
modern industry. A handful of sugar crystals
thrown into a vat of sorghum syrup makes the
whole mass, until then obdurate, crystallise at
once.

In the dispute between the Westport Coal
Company and its men, the court said:

"If work is slack and the men wish, the company is recommended to distribute the work
among the men rather than to discharge employés."

And again it said, "that so long as there are
efficient, capable men at Denniston out of work
the company shall employ these, either by contract or day labour . . . before the company calls for tenders from outsiders or em-
ploys outsiders."

As to these awards, the Secretary for Labour
makes the comment that they "affect principles
in the relation of employer and employed hither-
to considered as being entirely within the domain of private judgment and freedom of contract."

Arbitration does not remove the bottom evil of all in the labour world, the economic inequality of masters and men which makes a free contract impossible because one of the parties is not free; but it certainly adds a humanising touch to the methods of the struggle, and all civilisation is lifted a stage.

The workingman is certainly less at a disadvantage under a system in which he is guaranteed the right to be heard, and to be heard in public, than under the present capitalists' régime where he is so often refused any hearing, public or private.   The workers are safer before a Court of Arbitration than before a General Manager or a Board of Directors, or a general fixing wages by martial law.

The New Zealand court has but just touched in its decisions on the most important principle at issue in the regulation of wages—whether wages must follow prices or prices wages. Must wages be dependent on prices necessary to market commodities, or must these prices be dependent on the wages necessary to maintain the people in decent comfort?

The workingman's mind is evidently moving to the latter position.   Several of the greatest strikes of recent years, like the English coal strike of 1893, and the strike in Lord Penrhyn's quarries, have had the "living wage" for their inspiring principle, and this new position of the workingmen in those strikes received the open support of some of the most influential members of Parliament, newspapers, and even capitalists of Great Britain.

This doctrine seeks to make true the fiction of John Stuart Mill that wages are determined by the standard of living among the working-men. What John Stuart Mill said was the law of wages, the workingmen are seeking to bring about. The New Zealand law, the moment this new political economy that prices must follow wages invades the bench, can be made a powerful instrument in reinforcing the working-men. Decisions made by judges in industrial matters can usually be observed to be based not so much on "law" as on their notions of political economy.

A way in which the workingmen as voters could secure the introduction of compulsory arbitration is suggested by the Fabian Society in the tract to which we have just referred.

Local authorities can "make it a condition of the contract that all disputes between employer and workingmen shall be referred to arbitration" in contracts given out by them.

Important as the Conciliation Boards and Arbitration Courts of New Zealand are in their special field of labour troubles, they have an aspect even more important.   They are the only cheap, informal, speedy courts of justice which exist anywhere.   In these New Zealand courts alone do the people get a taste of that cheap and speedy justice of which they have always been dreaming, which the agitators, in the days of the Puritan Commonwealth, begged might be made to break forth out of the ground like a fountain. In these courts another field has been added to the social territory wrested from the region of private war and violence, and another baron or strong man has been harnessed to the collar of the common good.

The spirit of the law in this aspect is admirably voiced in a paragraph in Secretary Tregear's report for the Department of Labour in 1898.   In opposing the proposition that all the costs of the board should be charged to the disputing parties, Mr. Tregear said:

"Great care must be taken lest the usefulness of the acts be crippled by the fear of extreme expense.   In such cases, justice becomes a luxury only to be enjoyed by the rich, and the present merit of the act, namely, that it reaches down to remove the tiniest industrial irritant— would be lost.   It is better that the country should bear the slight expense attending the sitting of boards than that one citizen should have to say, 'I am oppressed and unjustly treated, but am not rich enough to make my complaint reach the ears of those in power; I must suffer in silence.' . . . The reproach often used in the past concerning courts of justice and the part played in them by the power of wealth should never be allowed to be cast upon the Court of Arbitration, and, although perhaps it may be idealistic to hope that one day justice may be dispensed free of charge to all, still in this matter the country may draw near the ideal by taking on itself the burden of its weaker members at a cost infinitesimal when divided among all, and it will be repaid by the steadiness with which the general level of industrial life will be sustained."

We all preach that the property and ability of each—the ten talents—exist for the service of all. That is the bottom doctrine of all civilisation. We open the oldest book we have, the "Precepts of Ptah Hotep," and we find it there. New Zealand practises it in a new field.

New Zealand has made the most important advance in the practical enforcement of this doctrine of the stewardship of wealth. It is the first to establish that, in this field of the relations of labour and capital, the steward is not to be left to himself to determine how he is to administer the trust.

Industries, it is a fundamental thought in this New Zealand legislation, are not individual creations; they are not made by the workingmen alone nor by capital alone, but are a social creation and subject to social control. Every manufacture, every investment, has been brought to where it is now by long ages of social effort. It is kept going to-day by the co-operation of all the people in countless ways, not the least among them the protection which the people gives, through the state.

If property is a trust, says the spirit of New Zealand legislation not only in this but in other laws, it is the interests of the ward that are paramount, not those of the trustee; the ward must have something to say, and the state must protect the ward and regulate the trustee.

The Compulsory Arbitration law of New Zealand and its laws for progressive taxation, land resumption, and labour regulation, are, in truth, the most advanced applications yet made in the modern world of the doctrines of Carlyle and Ruskin and all the great poets, that captains of industry are captains in the public service; that the labourers and the employer alike are social functionaries; that to labour and to lead labour are duties which no citizen has a right to disregard; that they who do not work, shall not eat, nor, says the Compulsory Arbitration law, shall they fight, which most men would rather do than eat.

The Compulsory Arbitration law is an attempt to realise in its field the loftiest teachings of the loftiest apostles of the religion of humanity, the religion of labour and love.

From the ideal point of view, it is a very crude attempt, a mere rudimentary beginning, but, from the practical point of view, it is one of the surest forward steps yet made by any people.

These people, by undertaking thus to enforce the social duties of industry, will be all the more likely to take the other steps that their new path will call for.   It is, for instance, imperative that they educate every citizen to industry, and that then they guarantee him the opportunity of industry.

Compulsory arbitration is only a step in that direction, but it is a step.   The greatest economic question involved in compulsory arbitration is, whether property and business shall be distributed by the methods of reason and brotherliness, or by the methods of force and mere greed; whether men shall have a fair chance according to their ability, enterprise, prudence and self-respect, or whether all the business chances shall go to the most unscrupulous and greedy, regardless of all other intellectual or moral qualities.

It is a question of the deepest force at work in the distribution of wealth; it is an economic question, economic all the more because it is also an ethical question.

New Zealand answers this question as the

progress of civilisation always has answered it. An act which seemed merely to contemplate peace in industry, if it proves permanently successful will turn out to be a powerful instrument in the democratisation of industry, the equalisation of economic conditions, the humanising of life, and the expansion of civilisation into a new world.

A genius, says Ralph Waldo Emerson, shows himself by carrying an existing idea or an institution a step farther than it had gone before. Many a man, he says, before him has taken the first, second or third steps. The genius which conceived and framed the Compulsory Arbitration law answers exactly to this description. It has taken the old institution of the court, the old ideas of peace and justice, and has carried them on into a new field. It has made no break with the past, but has developed all its familiar and venerable processes one step farther in their social evolution.

The establishment of a court in a field where only violence had been the judge before, the advance of the principles and institutions of civil law into social territory given over to anarchy, is always one of the great events. The emergence of the Geneva tribunal of 1872, above the troubled waters of international belligerency was such an event.

The Compulsory Arbitration law of New Zealand is such an event in a world of wars not less devastating than those between nations.   It is an event more entirely without precedent in the sphere of business, and of more startling interest than it would have been in the sphere of politics, if the powers in the Peace Congress at The Hague had set up an authority, as some peace congress some day will do, to forbid all war, and had clothed it with the force to make its prohibition good.   As soon as the majority of nations want international arbitration they will have it, but it can come only by compulsory arbitration as long as there is one nation fool enough or knave enough to prefer to fight.

Perhaps the greatest aspect of the law of New Zealand is this—that it "blazes the trail" along which international arbitration must move, if it would succeed.

We discover then that in New Zealand, in compulsory arbitration, we are dealing not merely with a novelty in a subordinate field of legislation, but with a new growth of the living organism of modern society.

There is only one Compulsory Arbitration law in the world, and that has been in operation only four years and in an isolated country, and we must not generalise too freely.   Similar laws might operate differently in different countries;

this law may still be crippled by sinister amendments moved by false friends.

Not forgetting this, let us sum up the results and tendencies of compulsory arbitration as evidenced in actual incidents of the industrial life of New Zealand, in the last four years:

1st. Strikes and lockouts have been stopped.

2d. Wages and terms have been fixed so that manufacturers can make their contracts ahead without fear of disturbance.

3d. Workingmen, too, knowing that their income cannot be cut down nor locked out, can marry, buy land, build homes.

4th. Disputes arise continually, new terms are fixed, but industry goes on without interruption.

5th. No factory has been closed by the act.

6th. The country is more prosperous than ever.

7th. The awards of the Arbitration Court fix a standard of living which other courts accept in deciding cases affecting workingmen.

8th. Awards made by compulsory arbitration are often renewed by a voluntary agreement when they expire.

9th. Trade-unions are given new rights, and are called upon to admit all competent workingmen in the trade.

10th. Compulsion in the background makes conciliation easier.

11th. Compulsory publicity gives the public, the real arbitrator, all the facts of every dispute.

12th. Salaried classes as well as wage-earners are claiming the benefits of arbitration.

13th. Peaceable settlement with their men has been made possible for the majorities of the employers who wanted to arbitrate, but were prevented by minorities of their associates.

14th. Labour and capital are being organised into trade-unions and associations instead of mobs and monopolists.

15th. Trade honesty is promoted by the exposure and prevention of frauds on the public.

16th. Humane and law-abiding business men seek the protection of the law to save themselves from destruction by the competition of inhumane and law-breaking rivals.

17th. The weak and the strong are equalised both among capitalists and the workingmen.

18th. The victory is given as nearly as possible to the right instead of to the strong, as in war.

19th. The concentration of wealth and power are checked.

20th. The distribution of wealth is determined along lines of reason, justice, and the greatest need, instead of along lines of the greatest greed.

21st. Democracy is strengthened by these equalisations.

22d. It furnishes the people their only cheap, speedy, and untechnical justice.

If the American people have any lesson to learn from these experiences of New Zealand, they can be trusted to learn it. The object of the writer has not been to enforce his views, but to present the facts of an interesting social experiment, on which the public could, if it chose, build views of its own.

Of course, "our circumstances are different." Our circumstances have not been so different but that they have developed the same evils. Perhaps they may develop the same remedy.

The New Zealanders have had several great advantages. They are a people of one race, and they are isolated. That they are united by race is an accident. Union can be also achieved by moral will, as doctors used to say of the healing of a wound, "by first intention," or "by immediate union," to use the newest phrase.

Men of almost every race have united to form the politics and society of these United States. Why can they not unite to reform them? And as for the isolation, that is a fortunate incident for the weak, but the United States has a nobler kind of isolation in its might and wealth. It can stand alone for any cause it chooses to espouse.